GOSPEL AND CULTURE

An Interaction between Christianity and Mizo Culture

H. Lalrinthanga

Christian World Imprints

First Published in 2020 by

Christian World Imprints
Christian Publishing & Books from India
C-3, Wazirpur Industrial Area
Delhi-110052
cwidelhi2017@gmail.com
www.ChristianWorldImprints.com
Phone: +91 11 41526079

ISBN: 978-93-5148-453-0 (HB)
ISBN: 978-93-5148-454-7 (PB)

Printed in India.

Contents

Acknowledgments

It is my pleasure to acknowledge the contribution of the Churches in Mizoram for the betterment of the Mizo society in different ways. With the introduction of Christianity in Mizoram, it brings a lot of changes in the Mizo society. Some of the Mizo traditional cultures were completely change, while other cultures were revive with modification form and introduced new cultures. This book is about the relationship of Christianity and culture in the twentieth century. This book sees that the Church is no longer against Mizo culture, but custodian of Christian faith and Mizo culture.

At the outset, I am indebted to express my sincere thanks to the Almighty God, who gave me an opportunity to do this work.

I would like to express my to my friend and colleaque who helped me in different ways. Special thanks to Prof. T. Vanlaltlani who always encourage me to make a publication.

I am really grateful to Rev. Prof. Vanlalnghaka Ralte, Principal of the Aizawl Theological College who has written preface for the book.

I also express my sincere thanks to Rev. Prof. Vanlalchhuanawma, a renounce historian, who has written foreword for the book.

I expressed my special thanks to my wife Lalrokimi, my daughter H. Lalvenhimi and my son Benjamin Lalrinkima, who constantly pray for me and encourage me with moral support.

H. Lalrinthanga
Aizawl Theological College

Preface

I feel honour and privilege to be invited by Rev. Dr. H. Lalrinthanga, my colleague and member of the faculty of Aizawl Theological College in the Department of History of Christianity, to write a preface to his book *Gospel and Culture: An Interaction between Christianity and Mizo Culture*. In this book the author has given a careful examination on the interaction between Christianity and Mizo culture after the introduction of Christianity in Mizoram.

The relationship between Christianity and Culture has been a subject of debate among the Mizo till today. Therefore, any serious research on this issue is important and appreciable. As a competent Mizo Christian historian, the author has sincerely expounded the subject with brevity, vividness and clarity.

The author has used quite a number of primary sources such as Church documents, Government documents, unpublished papers and research works which give depth to the research and make it priceless and reliable. The author has also made use of a number of secondary sources which strengthen and supplement the primary sources.

This invaluable research will certainly help the readers to have an in-depth knowledge about the relationship between Christianity and Culture in general and in the context of

Mizoram in particular. I do hope that this book will have a significant contribution to widen the horizons of our understanding of history of Christianity in the world.

Rev. Prof. Vanlalnghaka Ralte
Principal
Aizawl Theological College

Glossary

Kut	:	Festival
Jhum	:	Forest land burnt and cleared for paddy field
Tlawmngaihna	:	Mizo code of conduct
Hnatlang	:	Community work
Puithiam	:	Village priest
Salam	:	A fine paid by an offender
Zu	:	Rice-beer/Alcoholic beverages
Thingpui tam	:	A severe famine

Introduction

It humbles me to be invited to write forward to such crucial issue of Christianity-culture interface. Rina, my close colleague on the faculty of the Aizawl Theological College, who authors this book has his scholarship acknowledged by the Senate of Serampore College on church-state relationship in Mizo context. That tells upon the general acknowledgement of his competence in the analysis of religio-culture interplay. This dissertation is a by-product of his highly valued doctoral thesis on *Church and State Relationship in the Mizo Socio-Political Life 1952 to 2006.* Perfection is beyond anybody's reach while the author may be credited completeness in addressing every aspect of the subject in question.

In an attempt to study an interaction between Gospel and Culture this research work singles out *Kut* as a symbol of the entire Mizo cultural milieu. Christianity in Mizoram as is the case in other countries brings with it unprecedented changes in the whole socio-cultural scenario. Of the traditional cultural heritage *Kut* (Festival) is unique. It alone combines the moral, ethical, socio-economic and religious image of the people. Three of the *Kut* selected for this investigation include *Chapchar Kut* (Jhuming Festival - Spring Kut for fertility), *Mim Kut* (Maize Festival - Commemoration of the Deceased) and *Pawl Kut* (Harvest Festival – Thanksgiving *Kut).* All these *Kut* are accompanied with traditional feast, dance, singing and merry-making. On the introduction of Christianity they came to be strongly restricted and virtually done away with. Struggle to revive those *Kut* lately in the christianized Mizo society has been an epoch-making. Despite sincere efforts from various people groups to revive the *Kut* there still seems to be a widespread inhibition on the part of the large Christian public to endorse the trend. Factors for either rejection or approval of the *Kut*, the entire cultural heritage for that matter, are investigated and discussed.

Rina has made a tactful historical probe into the traditional values and cultural norms and practices employing a historico-analytical method, thus, viewing history from an indigenous perspective. The stated focus is "to see to what extent the traditional festivals came into Christian practices." A disquieting issue is that sincere aspirations to revive all the *Kut* has met with renewal of a modified *Chapchar Kut* only amidst serious doubts and critical remarks from the churches. Historical questions cited in the methodological consideration are duly investigated, such as, Why did the missionaries and the new converts condemn the traditional culture? Why did the church not appreciate the celebration of the festivals? What are the reasons for the recent re-introduction of *Chapchar Kut* festivals? What were some of the theological developments that had shaped in the celebration of festivals? Scholarly insights are provided.

Identification of the ongoing debate regarding the re-introduction of traditional *Kut* as well as the connected moral issues is eye-opening. Mixed responses to re-introduction of *Chapchar Kut* till date are critically analyzed. A close observation reveals that innate qualms in the psyché of the older generation of the churches' leadership vie with the more liberal approach of the younger generation. Rina in line with the contemporary mind-set proposes formalization of celebrating the traditional *Mizo Kut* to initiate Christian seasonal celebration of God and his creation. For anyone with Mizo Christian cultural genius reading of this book is a must.

Rev. Prof. Vanlalchhuanawma
Former Principal
&
Head of Deparment, History of Christianiy
Aizawl Theological College

Introduction
Methodological Consideration

This is an attempt to see the historical process of the interaction between Christianity and culture on the resurgence *Kut*, the traditional festival. *Kut* played very important role in the Mizo society, as they are the main symbolic and practical expression of the Mizo culture. The celebrations are largely related to religious belief systems. *Kut* have their own significance in different ways within the Mizo society. The Mizo celebrated three main *Kut* like *Chapchar Kut*, *Mim Kut* and *Pawl Kut* with different times and occasions. When Christianity was introduced in Mizoram, Christians condemned most of the cultural values as taboo, and the new converts abandoned the religious-cultural beliefs and practices including *Kut*. The conflict between traditional leaders and Christian converts came to such a point that it disrupted their cultural system and created chaos and confusion in the society. Since, India's Independence the new generation wanted to revive and renew these cultural traditional festivals and other cultural elements.

With the passage of time when Mizo had their own District in 1952, the government declared holidays of the celebration of *Kut*. Since then, *Kut* was celebrated in 1960-1962 by the government without any opposition from the church. But in 1964 celebration, untoward incident was happened, and this incident became the

Chapter 1

Mizo Traditional Values and Practices An Overview

In order to understand the nature and characteristic of the interaction between the Mizo culture and Christianity, it is necessary to be informed first about the socio-cultural and religious background of the people. In a tribal people the social, economic, political and religious life cannot be separated since they are connected each other.

The People

The term "Mizo" is a generic term and stand for all the different tribes or clans who inhabit the entire perimeter of the present Mizoram, and whose culture and traditions, similar are commonly designated by the term "Mizo."[1] The word "Mizo" literally means "Hill People" or "Highlander" (here *Mi* means people and *zo* means hill) consisting of several clans or sub-tribes such as Lusei, Hmar, Ralte, Pawih, Paihte, and other clans. The people who lived in Mizoram (at one point named Lushai Hill) called themselves "Mizo" from time immemorial, which covers all ethnic *Zo* people.[2] The first Superintendent of Mizoram, J. Shakespear also states that "Mizo" was the commonly used for the common identity of the people inhabiting the region.[3] Today, the term "Mizo" is used in a wider sense, not only for the inhabitant of Mizoram but also for who live in the neighbouring states and countries.

The Land

The state of Mizoram is a hilly region lying between latitude 21 56' and 24 31' North and longitude 92 16' and 93 26' East. The Tropic of Cancer runs through the heart of the land. It covers an area of 21, 090 sq. km. Chittagong Hill Tracts of Bangladesh and the Tripura state bound it on the north, Cachar District of Assam and Manipur state on the south, Chin and Arakan Hills of Myanmar on the west. When the British annexed the region, it formed one administrative district under the name of the Lushai Hills District in 1898 and was made a part and parcel of Assam state. In 1954, by an Act of Parliament, the name of the territory was changed from Lushai Hills to Mizo District in April 1954 and it was enacted from September 1954. In 1972, it was upgraded to the status of Union Territory, and the name was also changed to Mizoram. Finally, Mizoram was conferred to the Statehood in 1986 by the Indian Government and became the 23rd state in the Indian Union.

Political Life

In the traditional Mizo society inter-village warfare was very common. Therefore, in order to maintain security, all the Mizo villages were built on hill tops. Each village has its own Chief and ruled with the help of the council of elders. The elders were appointed by the Chief himself. The Chief was the supreme authority in the village. All the cases were brought to the consent of the Chief and no one could refuse the judgment of the Chief. According to Selet Thanga, one of the Mizo writers, Chiefs can be classified into two groups. The first group was those who ruled tyrannically upon their subjects, such Chiefs did not want anyone who could compete with their chieftainships. The second group was those who ruled for the benefits of their subjects.[4] The good Chiefs acted as a father to their subjects; they helped them when they were in distress and if the Chiefs got into any difficulties they in turn helped the Chiefs.[5] One of the Superintendents of the Lushai Hills, N. E. Parry also believes that the villagers could check too much arbitrary use of power, because the Mizo are accustomed to migrate freely from village to village, and a Chief who disregards the customs and oppressed the villagers would speedily lose the bulk of subjects.[6] McCall, the Administrator of the then Lushai Hills observes that all the system of community obligation existed under the term *Tlawmngaihna*,[7] implying public service.

Social Life

The traditional Mizo society was a close-knit society. The village society was cohesive and would meet in community feasts that took place after animal sacrifice performed by villagers or after a successful community hunting. The acts of decency and courtesy were considered to form norms of good conduct in the society. Showing reverence to elders was one among the many acts of decency, which the children were required to learn. In the Mizo society, the system called *Hnatlang*, which means communal labour in which everyone is expected to take part, was very strong. Construction of village path, construction of roads to the *jhum*[8] cultivation, construction of community hall, preparations of water points were done by the community. The villagers were expected to contribute labour for the welfare of the community and each family was under obligation.[9]

If any villager was sick and was unable to do the most laborious task of preparing *jhum* cultivation, the neighbours would readily come forward lending helping hands to do the work for the needy. If a villager was short of rice, those having plenty would readily share the same with the needy.

Economic Life

In the traditional Mizo society, as they had no monitary system, the barter system was in practice. Exchange of things was done in terms of kinds. Among the Mizo the value of property was judged in terms of *Sial* (Mithun).[10] Therefore, *Sial* played a very important role in the social was well as in the economic life of the Mizo. Even the bride price was determined in term of *Sial*.

The principal means of livelihood of the people is based on agriculture in which *jhuming* or shifting cultivation was practices. As there is no flat land for productive cultivation, *jhuming* or slash and burn method is the only possible cultivation method. This is the most common method of cultivation and agricultural, products like paddy, maize, ginger, chillies, tobacco, and other crops are grown in the *jhum*. Though the Mizo economic condition was always unsecured, J. Shakespear said that the Mizo had remained satisfied by meeting the bare necessity for their day-to-day lives.

Religious Life

In a close-knit society of the Mizo, it is difficult to determine what is religious and what is not religious. Here, we are trying to identify the Mizo belief before the introduction of Christianity.

Mizo Sakhua

The pre-christian social life of the Mizo was dominated by their religious beliefs. It is difficult to give an exact meaning of religion. There are number of definitions of religion. The Mizo religion also had different versions. J. H. Lorrain, one of the missionaries gives four meaning for Mizo *sakhua*: (a) an object of worship, a god, (b) ancient ancestors who are worshipped by the Lushais, (c) the spirit who presides over the house or household, (d) religion, religious rites and ceremonies.[11] It shows that Lorrain was the first one who translated Mizo *sakhua* as religion. Liangkhaia, one of the Mizo writers believes that the two words *Sa* and *Khua* were eventually combined and became *Sakhua*, which is now a term used for religion.[12] However, the research team of the Tribal Research Institute caution us that *sa* and *khua* should not be separated too clearly as Liangkhaia does.

Lalsawma, another Mizo writer believes that the English word 'Religion' should not be translated by the Mizo word *Sakhua*, because the term *Sakhua* was used for a specific rite over with the spirits of the jungle.[13] Lalsangkima Pachuau also goes along with Lalsawma by saying that. "There is no doubt that *Sakhua* was an essential part of the Mizo primal religion, but it did not constitute the whole religion."[14] Hence, Hrangkhuma Fanai, one of the Senior Baptist Church Pastors prefers to use the term 'beliefs' instead of the word 'religion' because according to him "not all Mizo 'beliefs' were religious characters."[15]

Then, what is the Mizo religion? Most of the English writers like McCall (1949),[16] E. Chapman and Clark (1968),[17] J. M. Lloyd,[18] and others described the Mizo religion as 'animism.' Mizo writers like Zairema,[19] Saiaithanga[20] and Challiana[21] also accepted the Mizo religion was animism. Another group of Mizo writers believe that although the Mizo religion was often called animism in its character but it is only to offer sacrifice to appease the deity. Therefore, they argued that the Mizo religion was not animistic. Lalsawma indicates that the word "Primal Religion" is much more appropriate expression of the Mizo religion rather than "Animism."[22] Liangkhaia also argues that Mizo *Sakhua* was not animistic.[23]

In the above discussion, we have two different opinions about the Mizo religion, whether it was animism or not. Then, what is animism? The word "animism" is taken from the Latin word *anima*, which means soul. Prominent exponent of the animistic theory is Edward B. Taylor (1832-1917) who found animism as the earliest form of religion among the primitive. According to him, animism is a belief in the existence of spiritual beings or spirits.[24] As per this belief or theory of animism, all living beings or natural objects have spirit or soul (*anima*). Soul is recognized as the animating principle of all life. These spirits are believed to be invisible forces or powers that prevail and operate in the nature.[25] Thus, according to Taylor, animism "includes the belief in souls and in a future state, these doctrines practically resulting in some kind of active worship."[26] The Mizo traditional religious belief falls into the above definition of animism. They lived in constant fear of evil spirits and offered sacrifices to appease them. And also believed in the existence of one Supreme Being, a good God who does not need to be feared and so partially ignored. Their object of worship was mainly to appease the evil spirits.

Concept of God

The Mizo believed in the existence of One Supreme Being called *Pathian*, creator of everything, who does not harm human beings, who had, however, little concern with human beings. They believed that he lived somewhere above and as such called him *Chung Pathian*, meaning "God of above." There were also certain other high beings such as *Vanchung Nula*, means "Maiden in Heaven," *Khuanu* (means Mother Cosmos or cosmic goddess) and *Pu Vana* (literally means "grandfather heaven" or "heavenly father"). According to Zaithanga, the word *Pathian* can be correctly translated as "Holy Father," for *Pa* means "father" and *thian* means "holy." *Pathian* and these other beings were not worshipped, and sacrifices were never offered to them. Therefore, they conceived the idea that they need not offer sacrifices to him. Their idea about God was almost the same from the Christian ideas of God. In the words of Sangkima, "The only difference is that in those early days they did not have a clear conception of God's personality as the Christians have today."[27]

Mizo also believed in the existence of *Khuavang*, a divinity directly concerned with human affairs, the determinant of fates and destiny. If things go wrong they used to say, "My *Khuavanga* is bad" and if things are in their favour they also used to say "My *Khuavang* is good."

Concept of Spirit

The Mizo 'do not worship the sun or the moon or any of the force of nature,'[28] but they believed that the existence of evil spirits, which were commonly called *Ramhuai*. They were identified with different names. They also believed that various evil spirits called *Huai* inhabited hill, stream, big stone, cave, tree, etc. These spirits, however, were not beneficent, cruel, malicious and capricious.[29] All types of calamities, failure of crops, ill health, disease, death and other misfortunes were attributed to the evil spirits. *Puithiam*[30] prescribed according to the nature and magnitude of the distress, what particular sacrifices was necessary to appease the spirit. At this, a member of the clan sacrificed pigs, fowls and other domestic animals or birds whatever asked by the *Puithiam*.

The Concept of Life After Death

J. Shakespear has given the first written account of the Mizo concept of life after death. In his book *The Lusei-Kuki Clan*, he writes,

> The Lushais believe in a spirit world beyond the grave, which is known as *Mi-thi-khua*, i.e., the abode of departed spirit-but on the far side of *mi-thi-khua* runs the *Pial* river, beyond which lies *Pial-ral*, an abode of bliss. Access to this is not obtained by a life of virtue while on the earth, but the due performance of sacrifices and the killing of men and certain animals in the courts of Venus.[31]

According to the general belief, *Mitthi Khua* was meant for the ordinary people who could not perform certain sacrifice during their lifetime. It was believed that the life in *Mitthi Khua* were to be a shadow of what they possessed in the earthly life. Life was full of misery and anxiety. They undergo pains and hurts; desire for something better and they worked, ate, and slept.

Another place where dead soul abode was called *Pialral* (the Paradise), lies beyond the *Pial* river. According to the general belief, only the souls of the rich, who performed *Thangchhuah*,[32] could go to *Pialral*. Those who went there would not have to work, but enjoyed a plentiful of ready-husked rice, meat and *zu* (rice beer).

The Mizo believed that the soul of the death wanders in the vicinity of the village for about three months. During this period the family would not occupy the usual seat of the deceased at the family meal and set aside some food for him or her. After three months the soul is believed to have left the village and begun its journey to *Mitthi Khua*. On the way to *Mitthi Khua* the soul passes through different stages. First the soul passes the *Rih* Lake, which is situated to the east of Mizoram. After that the soul reached the beautiful place called *Hringlangtlang* from which the spirit of the departed look back and view with longing the world, relatives and friends that they had left behind. In due course of time, the spirit reaches a spring called *Lungloh Tui* and drinks the water, and at the same time it plucks and wears the beautiful flower *Hawilo Par* (the flower of no turning back) in their hair and ears. This makes the soul loses it desire to return to the world and then they forget all about human beings. Finally, the spirit approaches to *Mitthi Khua*.

Community Sacrifices

The Mizo had two important community sacrifices. They are *Kawngpui Siam* and *Fano Dawi*, which were closely related to the festivals. The following discussion shows how the Mizo performed the community sacrifices.

Kawngpui Siam

Kawngpui Siam was a ceremony performed before the *Chapchar Kut*. "This was an annual sacrifice which was offered to all the spirits to ensure prosperity for the whole village especially in hunting and trapping wild animals and also for their safety from enemies and raiders."[33] The village Chief priest performed it with some of the elders. They brought rice-beer with them in a bamboo tube and in a gourd, which was consumed on the spot with the meat sacrificed animal except the intestines of the animal, killed which was offered to the spirit. A place was cleared on each side of this place and a cane was hung up between them across the road. The *Puithiam* then sacrifices a pig and calls all the animals of the jungle except the tiger.

On this day no one was allowed to go out of the village and no strangers were allowed to enter the village and if there were any outsiders they were asked to go elsewhere. Absentees were liable to a fine of *salam*.[34] In the early morning, they go to look at the ashes, and are supposed to be able to see the likeness to footprints of the animals. They were to kill in the chase. If a man's footprints were seen, it was unfortunate, for he would be killed.

Fano Dawi

Fano Dawi was another ceremony performed by the Mizo. "This was an annual sacrifice for the whole village which was performed for protection of the young and growing paddy plants and their safety from destruction caused by wild animals and birds."[35] It was usually held in the month of July. "The chief prepares *zu* in his house.

Puithiam and two elders go just outside the village on the road to the *jhum* and sacrifice a cock, and its wings are hung on either side of the road and parts of a sacrificed animal or fowl dedicated to the God or spirit to whom it was offered is placed in the middle of the road."[36] On the day of *Fano Dawi*, no one leave the village or go to the fields or to husk rice except to carry water. A clack cock is sacrificed which is provided in alternate years by the *ramhual upa*[37] and the Chief.

Propitiatory Sacrifices

As an effort to heal the sick several sacrifices were performed by a priest by offering domestic animals such as pigs, dogs, chickens and goats, in each village a *Sadawt* was available to perform sacrifices to the evil spirits that caused diseases and affliction.

Different kinds of animals were sacrificed as prescribed by the priest, for different kinds of sacrifices. The Welsh Foreign Mission Report in 1898-1899 clearly shows the Mizo practice of sacrifices and the functions of a priest, the Report says,

> Any sickness, which they cannot understand, is attributed to evil Spirit, and sometimes, if a man meets with great afflictions, they acknowledge the hands of god. No meat is eaten by them but that is sacrifice to the Evil spirit, and many families have sacrificed what animals they possessed to appease their anger. A priest is to be found in almost every village, and it is he that looks after the sacrifices.[38]

J. M. Lloyd believes that sacrifices gradually lost its meaning. According to him, in the sacrificial ceremonies, "there would be no congregational participation, no prayers were offered, no hymn sung, certainly no sermon would be preached!"[39] In view of this, Zairema raises the question on whether these sacrifices could strictly be termed 'religious.' According to him, the sacrifices had two natures; the sacrifice to the evil spirit were non-obligatory because only the rich people afford to perform them regularly, while the poor people could do so only in serious situation like long illness. Obligatory sacrifices were to be performed at birth, puberty, marriages and regular festivals. These were considered as real sacrifices or gifts and prayers to the deity.[40]

Family Rites

As there were many clans among the Mizo, so there were many *Sakhua* spirits, each responsible for a particular clan over which it ruled. The Mizo worshipped their respective *Sakhua* in order to receive blessings.[41] A *Puithiam* of the clan performed all the sacrifices, and only the member of his family can be present. The *Puithiam* taught the chants of the rites to his sons who were to continue his work.

Concluding Remarks

The above discussion of the socio-religious context of the Mizo before the Christian era indicated that the Mizo were rich in cultural activities. Their social, political, economic and religious system was related to one another. Although Christianity abolished some of their cultures, some still survived and others modified to relate to Christianity.

End Notes

1 Sangkima, *Mizos: Society and Social Change 1890-1947* (Guwahati: Spectrum Publications, 1992), 3. Hereafter cited as Sangkima, *Mizos: Society and Social Change 1890-1947.*

2 Vumson, *Zo History* (Aizawl: The Author, n.d.), 2.

3 J. Shakespear, *The Lusei Kuki Clan,* Part I (Aizawl: Tribal Research Institute, 1975), introduction. Hereafter cited as Shakespear, *The Lusei Kuki Clan.*

4 Selet Thanga, *Pi Pu Lenlai*, 13th ed., (Aizawl: Lianchhungi Book Store, 1990), 3. Hereafter cited as Thanga, *Pi Pu Lenlai.*

5 Chhangte Lal Hminga, *The Life and Witness of the Churches in Mizoram* (Serkawn: Literature Committee, Baptist Church of Mizoram, 1987), 27. Hereafter cited as Hminga, *The Life and Witness of the Churches in Mizoram.*

6 N. E. Parry, *A Monograph on Lushai Customs and Ceremonies*, reprinted (Shillong: Ri Khasi Offset Printers, 1988), 1, 2. Hereafter cited as Parry, *Lushai Customs and Ceremonies.*

7 *Tlawmngaihna*: It is a unique possession, the pride and glory of the Mizo. It comprises a wide spectrum of the social virtues such as charity, diligence, patience, bravery, loving kindness, and unselfish sacrifice of one's service to

the welfare of the community in all spheres of life. See Challiana, *Pi Pu Nun* (Aizawl: Lalrinliana & Sons, 1987), 9. Hereafter cited as Challiana, *Pi Pu Nun*.

8 Jhum: Every year Mizo cut the jungles, burn the dried trunks and leaves and then till the soil for the paddy fields.

9 A. C. Ray, *States of Our Union Mizoram* (Delhi: Publications Division, Ministry of Information and Broadcasting Government of India, 1972), 10, 11.

10 Sangkima, *Mizos: Society and Social Change 1890-1947*, 49.

11 J. H. Lorrain, *Dictionary of the Lushai Language*, 4th reprint (Calcutta: The Asiatic Society, 1997), 401. Hereafter cited as Lorrain, *Dictionary of the Lushai Language*.

12 Liangkhaia, *Mizo Chanchin*, 5th ed. (Aizawl: L.T.L. Publication, 2002), 49. Hereafter cited as Liangkhaia, *Mizo Chanchin*.

13 Lalsawma, *Revivals-the Mizo Way* (Aizawl: The Author, 1994), 23. Hereafter cited as Lalsawma, *Revivals-the Mizo Way*.

14 Lalsangkima Pachuau, "Mizo Sakhua Then and Now: Change and Continuity between Mizo Primal Religion and Mizo Christianity," Faculty Research Seminar paper, UTC, November 12, 2003.

14 Hrangkhuma, "Mizoram Transformation Change…,"

16 Anthony Gilchrist McCall, *Lushai Chrysalis* (London: Lusac & Co., Limited, 1949), 67. Hereafter cited as McCall, *Lushai Chrysalis*.

17 E. Chapman & M. Clark, *Mizo Miracle*, edited by Marjorie Skyes (Madras: The Christian Literature Society), 11.

18 J. Meirion Lloyd, *History of the Church in Mizoram, Harvest in the Hill* (Aizawl: Synod Publication Board, 1991), 9. Hereafter cited as Lloyd, *History of the Church in Mizoram*.

19 Zairema, "The Mizos and their Religions," in *Towards A Tribal Theology: the Mizo Perspective*, edited by K. Thanzauva (Jorhat: Mizo Theological Conference, 1989), 33. Hereafter cited as Zairema, "The Mizos and their Religions."

20 Saiaithanga, *Mizo Sakhua* (Aizawl: Maranatha Press, 1984), 1.

21 Challiana, *Pi Pu Nun*.

22 Lalsawma, *Revivals- the Mizo Way*, 24.

23 Liangkhaia, *Mizo Chanchin*, 50.

24 Edward B. Taylor, "Animism," in *Reader in Comprehensive Religion An Anthropological Approach*, 3rd ed., edited by William A. Lessa and Evon Z. Vogt (New York: Harper & Row Publishers, 1972), 11. Hereafter cited as Taylor, "Animism".

25 Anand Spencer, *Understanding Religion: Theories and Methodology* (Patiala: Vision and Venture, 1997), 165.

26 Taylor, "Animism," 11.

27 Sangkima, *Mizos: Society and Social Change 1890-1947*, 52.

28 Shakespear, *The Lusei Kuki Clan*, 61.

29 Lloyd, *History of the Church in Mizoram*, 9.

30 Puithiam: The *Puithiam* is the village priest. He is remunerated for his service in paddy. The system of remuneration varies in different villages and is again a matter of local arrangement. See Parry, *Lushai Customs and Ceremonies*, 7.

31 Shakespear, *The Lusei Kuki Clan*, 62.

32 Thangchhuah: The title given to a man who has distinguished himself by killing a certain number of different animals in the chase, or by giving a certain number of public feasts.

33 *Zu in Mizo Society* (*Past and Present*) (Aizawl: Senior Research Officer, Tribal Research Institute, 1983), 16. Hereafter cited as, *Zu in Mizo Society*.

34 Salam: "A fine which when paid is divided among the chief and the elders of a village for their trouble in setting a case-generally five rupees or a pig of that value. This is killed and eaten by the chief and elders." See Lorrain, *Dictionary of the Lushai Language*, 401.

35 *Zu in Mizo Society*, 16.

36 Shakespear, *The Lushei Kuki Clan*, 80.

37 Ramhual Upa: These are the people who advise where jhums should be cut each year ans are allowed first choice of fields to cultivate. In consideration of their getting first choice of jhums, they have to pay heavier Fathang to the chief than ordinary villagers. See Parry, *Lushai Customs and Ceremonies*, 7.

38 K. Thanzauva, comp., *Reports of the Foreign Mission of the Presbyterian Church of Wales on Mizoram 1894-1957* (Aizawl: The Synod Literature and Publication Boards, 1997), 4.

39 Lloyd, *History of the Church in Mizoram*, 10.

40 Zairema, "The Mizos and their Religions," 34.

41 Shakespear, *The Lusei Kuki Clan*, 61, 62.

Chapter 2

The Mizo Traditional Festivals

Mizo had a number of community feasts and festivals, which were performed at a specific time and season of the year. The main *Kut* are *Chapchar Kut* (festival of spring), *Mim Kut* (festival performed when the crops other than paddy is first reaped), and *Pawl Kut* (harvest festival).

Origin of *Kut*

The origin of the Mizo *Kut* is not known clearly. Some writers hold the view that *Kut* originated from *Thlanrawkpa*, a famous legend of feasts.[1] According to B. Lalthangliana, one of the Mizo writers, *Kut* had been observed when the Mizo lived in Myanmar during their migration to their present habitat and more specifically while they stayed between *Run* River and *Tiau* River in the period between 1450 and 1750 AD.[2]

Origin of Chapchar *Kut*

The word *Chapchar* is composed of two words, *Chap*, which means bamboo, tree, or other jungle cut down and awaiting to be burned for *jhuming*; and *Char*, means dried up to the sun. All the Mizo writers and historians could not tell the exact time of the origin of *Chapchar Kut*. Some writers believe that it was originated when the Mizo lived in *Thantlang* village around 1480 A.D. during their migration from Kabaw valley.[3] Some hold they view that it was originated from *Suai tlang* under the Kawlni chief.[4] Some writers believe that it was originated while the Mizo lived between *Run* River and *Tiau* River.[5]

A commonly accepted legend told the origin of *Chapchar Kut*. According to the legend, when the Mizo lived in the famous village of Suai, one fine spring morning, the Chief gathered his village young men for hunting expedition into the deep forests to hunt for wild animals. The hunting expedition took several days. The villagers anxiously waited for their successful return with the expectancy. Feasting with meat and drinking of rice-beer and general rejoicing would follow that it.

After long and tiresome hunting, "The Chief and his desperadoes were not blessed by Chawngtinleri (the guardian Queen of the beasts) or they were cursed by Black Hollock by sprinkling its droppings on them."[6] The hunters came back to the village empty-handed and without any trophy. They were filled with shame and disappointment. The worthy young Chief's initiative and inventiveness had a bright idea.

To cover up their shame and discomfiture, the Chief arranged feast instantly. He offered a pig and asked his hunting-mates to contribute a fowl each. The entire community was invited to participate in the feast. The community joined by bringing pots of rice-beers. A feast was thus made with a plenty of meat and rice-beer. The mood was change from disappointment to joyful merrymaking. Young men and women threw hands around each other and danced in a circle; some singing and clapping hands all the while. The entire community enjoyed themselves even more than they would have done so if the hunters had come back successfully. The turned 'defeat into victory' as it were, and the *Chapchar Kut* was born. Since then, every year around that fateful time, Suai villagers repeated the festival of a sort. Many other villages followed with their own innovations and suitable time.[7]

Origin of Mim Kut

Mim Kut was a festival in honour of dead. As the family used to lament or weep for the departed ones in the family, *Mim Kut* was also called 'Feast of Weeping.'[8] Most of the Mizo history writers tell us the origin of *Mim Kut*. The story of the origin of *Mim Kut* reads like this,

> Tradition connects the origin of *Mim Kűt* to a couple named Ngama and Tlingi who falls in love and got married. But soon after Tlingi, the wife, died. On the death of his beloved wife, Ngama wept and wept, and one day while weeping he felt into a state of trance and said to have visited the *Mitthi Khua* (the village of the dead) and met his beloved wife Tlingi but found her famished. When asked about the reason Tlingi replied that she could not procure enough food to eat, and asked Ngama to go back and collect maize, cucumber, vegetables, etc., from the *jhum* and make offerings to her so that she might get things to eat her satisfaction. Ngama did everyting [sic] accordingly. After sometime, in (*an*) autumn month, Ngama was again in a state of trance. This time he saw Tlingi very stout and lovely. When he asked her the reason Tlingi told him that she became fat (*stout*) because of the offerings he made for her. Ngama, after recovering, told his friends all what he had experienced. It is stated that from that time onwards offerings to the death became a common practice.[9]

Hence, *Mim Kut* came to be celebrated as a festival to offer fruits and vegetables for the departed soul in the family.

Origin of Pawl Kut

Pawl means "straw," hence *Pawl Kut* was a *Kut* held soon after the harvest. According to Sangkima, two explanations are found as to the origin of *Pawl Kut*. The first explanation gave its origin with catching of *zu pawl* (one kind of wild rats especially found on *jhum* during harvest) found in the heap of straw, long ago when the Mizo were living in Myanmar. The second explanation connected the origins of *Pawl Kut* to the great famine called *Thingpui Tam*[10] which visited the Mizo when they were in the Kabaw Valley, for the three consecutive years.[11] During this famine people died and a number of people migrated from their villages.

On the fourth year they were relieved of the disaster by the blessing of what they called *Khawzim Pathian* (an old Lushai name for God or Providence). One day the chief suggested to his elders that they should prepare a public feast for thanksgiving in which all the people might enjoy meal to their heart's content. This was agreed by the elders. Therefore, on the next day, they arranged public feast where everybody would participate by killing fowls, pigs and goats. From this event there came into existence the *Pawl Kut*.[12]

Celebration of *Kut*

The nature of the celebration of *Kut* was differed from one another. The elements that involved in the celebration were almost the same. Detail accounts of the celebration of *Kut* may be summarized under the following.

Celebration of Chapchar Kut

The *Chapchar Kut* or spring festival was one of the most important and famous festivals of the Mizo. The *Chapchar Kut* celebration was held every year when the Mizo finished the *jhum* preparation for the paddy fields. It had usually taken place in the month of March or at the beginning of the spring. As most of the Mizo were agriculturist, they used to cut down the jungle annually for the paddy crops. The respite between the jungle cutting operation and the burning of *jhum* becomes all the more enjoyable in the spring time when the cold spell of winter yields to the spring and the trees and shrubs put out fresh leaves and flowers blossom. The *Chapchar Kut* celebration is perhaps the most joyful of Mizo *Kut*, as it is, with great fan-fare and merriment.[13] Thus, for the hard-working Mizo villagers, this is the rare respite they could enjoy leisurely in a year. The general celebration of the *Chapchar Kut* lasted for about four or five days, but its duration depended chiefly on the amount of *zu* (rice-beer) available in the village. The villagers would brew *zu* in advance. Young men and women as well as children would collect and prepare their respective *zu* (*zulawm*).

On the first day of the celebration, the members of the Chief's clan slaughter a pig for the feast, drinking rice-beer and that would follow a feast. This day was called *Lusei vawk talh ni* which literally means the day on which the Lushei killed their pigs. They would slaughter the pigs late in the day so that by the time the feast is ready most urchins would be a sleep. Elders spent the day drinking *zu*.

The next day this was done by the Ralte clan and followed other clans in the village for the village feast. They never killed *Vawkpa Sutnghak*[14] without any religious performance.[15] After the *Sadawt* (priest) chanted the religious rites, the pig would be killed. In the evening all the mothers and children would dress up in their best and would gather to perform *Chhawnghnawt*[16] by bringing with them rice, boiled eggs and meat, either in the village square or near the memorial platforms of the departed situated just outside the village. They would give tit bits to their friends and all would drink rice-beer.

On the night of the third day, young men and women dressed in their necklaces or amber, ear-rings of ivory and beautiful headgears, would gather together and performed traditional dance called *Chai*. They would form a circle in which the young men would have their arms across the women who would be interspersed alternate between the boys. Within the circle would be the drummer or gong beater, who would chant while the young people would sing and move slowly keeping time with the song. During the dance, the children of the village would go on serving rice-beer in bamboo cups to the dancing men and women.[17] As a custom, those who did not sing, dance or drink rice-beer throughout the day and night were not allowed to perform *Chai* dance in the ensuing days.

The next day is known as *Zupui ni*, which was a day of drinking rice-beer. *Zupui* is a rice-beer brewed with husks. It is a mild beer, specially brewed for festive and special days. One can drink *Zupui* for the whole day and not get drunk. *Zupui* is normally drunk with siphon or pipe immersed into the beer-pot. On this day *Zupui* contributed by various families were passed around the whole day. Towards the evening cultural sing-song and dancing would commence lasting till the small hours of the next morning, depending on the mood of the participants.

On the fifth day, it was customary to try and finish all the rice-beer contributed or collected for *Chapchar Kut*. The dance would continue day and night. The last day of the feast is known as "a day of rest" after eating and drinking. On this day people observed *hrilh*.[18] Going out on this day for work or hunting outside the village perimeter was 'taboo.' It was a common belief that a tiger would devour any one going into the jungles on these days.

Celebration of Mim Kut

The *Mim Kut* was celebrated at the end of August or in the beginning of September after the harvest of maize. It lasts, at the most for two days. At the beginning of the entire month for *Mim Kut*, the Chief and elders fixed the date for the celebration. On the eve of *Mim Kut*, all the family collected maize, cucumber, watermelon and other vegetables for the sacrifice to the dead. On the day of *Kut*, a raised platform made of bamboo near the kitchen would be cleaned and, cooked food with fresh vegetables and maize would be served on the platform for the soul of the dead ones to come and partake of the food so offered. The food offered would lie there for the next two or three days. The relatives of the dead were expected to partake of this food. "The breads for the dead were made with the even number while the bread for the live as odd number."[19] After three days the articles that were offered were eaten. The common belief was that after three days the departed soul was going to the village of the dead. The young men did not touch the offerings as they regarded it as 'taboo.'[20]

During *Mim Kut* celebration, rice-beer was consumed with much singing of the mourning songs in the house of one who had recently died. The songs invariably speak of the dear ones who had departed.

At the end of *Kut* celebration there would be a one-day holiday. The *Mim Kut* was a ceremony meant for the dead; therefore, it had certain religious significance apart from the social.

Celebration of Pawl Kut

Pawl Kut was a festival of harvest thanksgiving. This *Kut* was celebrated sometime in December or January after the harvest is over. *Pawl Kut* used to be a one day festival. The Chief and elders announced the date for the celebration of the *Kut* five days before the celebration. In the beginning the rice-beer was prepared by every family. The young men would go on hunting with a hope to trap animals and birds. In this occasion, the grandparent used to give *ar mit rawh*[21] to their grandchildren. The children used to wear the feather of the sacrificed.[22]

The Sailo (Chief clan) slaughtered pig for the first two days and the next day other clan would also kill as the same as in the celebration of *Chapchar Kut*. Every clan used their *Sadawt* for killing pigs.[23] *Pawl Kut* celebration for mainly children, but young men and women also participated freely. Children dressed in their finest clothes and ornaments. Children, young men and women collected stems or grain out of hay that had been unnoticed in the field. They would also go from door to door asking villagers to part with a little grain for making rice-beer. If they were given, they blessed the giver to long life and if they did not give, they curse them.

Children prepared rice-beer but they would not drink, but gave it to their elders in exchange for something. During *Pawl Kut*, even the poorest in the village would also eat meat and egg was a compulsory item. As in *Chapchar Kut*, mothers and children would gather at the outskirts of a villager bringing with them plates of rice, eggs and meat and feed one another. This is called *chhawnghnawt*. The young men and women would also join in the *chhawnghnawt*. The men would gather in the house of well-to-do person and would fellowship over a pot of rice-beer. The festival was followed by a day of rest. No work would be done on this day except the essential household tasks.

Elements of Traditional Festivals

This section deals with the discussion on the elements of the Mizo traditional festivals.

Zu (Rice-beer)

In the book, *Zu In Mizo Society*, clearly gives the importance of *zu* in the Mizo society, it reads.

> *Zu* played an important role in the early Mizo society and had been drunk on all important occasions. Without *zu* no ceremonies and religious function could be performed.[24]

The above quotation clearly stated that *zu* (rice-beer) played a very important role in every sphere of the life of the Mizo. They usually drank on the occasions of *Chapchar Kut*, *Mim Kut*, *Pawl Kut*, sacrificial and ceremonial functions. Young men and women drank *zu* only on the festivals. In the olden days, though *zu* was free for the adult people yet none of them ever drank excessively to lose his self-control. People condemned and contempt crying and tottering in the street due to intoxication. None of them liked to be admonished and be contempt by the public and tried to avoid it as far as they could. If not so, a group of young men would beat the addicts and drunkards under the cover of darkness.[25] Therefore, young men hardly drank *zu* except on the occasions of the celebration of festivals. Hence, we may say that before the spread of Christianity in Mizoram *zu* drinking was very common and was connected with the celebration of festivals and other occasions.

Dances

In the Mizo society, one of the important social lives was dances. The Mizo have a number of folk and community dances, which were inherited from generation to generation. In the olden days, dances were performed only on certain occasions and they were principal entertainments in the village. Some of the common dances of the past era are *Chai*, *Sakei Lu lam*, *Khual lam*, *Cheraw*, *Rallu lam* and *Chheih lam*. Each has its own significant in the life of the Mizo. As *Chai* dance was related to festivals special discussion will be given.

Chai is a dance performed only in the celebration of *Chapchar Kut*.[26] Therefore, *Chai* dance had a close connection with *Chapchar Kut*, in this dance, men and women stand alternately in a circle, with women holding on to the waist of the men, and the men on to the women shoulder. In the middle of the circle are the musicians who play the drum and the gong. The dancers sway to and fro and while the drummer and the gong man beat their instruments, they sway their feet to the tune of the *Chai* song sung in chorus. The dancers used to consume *zu* continuously while dancing.

Songs

"Before coming to the present habitat, Mizo while living in Burma had composed different kinds of folk songs. These include *Dar Hla*, *Bawh Hla*, *Chai Hla*, *Chawngchen Zai*, *Naupang Hla*, *Nauawih Hla*, *Sakhua* and *Inthawina Hla*."[27] According to Zatluanga, Mizo writer, there are nine different *Chai* songs, namely *Kawlni Chai Hla*, *Thailungi Zai*, *Mangkhaia Zai*, *Lallula* (Zopui) *Zai*, *Neihlaia Zai*, *Lera Zai*, *Chhim Zai*, *Darlung Zai* and *Lalvunga Zai*.[28] These songs were the most popular song, which people sung together with dancing as the time of *Chapchar Kut* celebration.

Mizo loved to sing and they sing on all happy and sad occasions. They sung at the time of celebration of *Chapchar Kut* with dance. They sung at the bereaved family during the celebration of *Mim Kut*. R. L. Thanmawia says, "The Mizo traditional tunes are very soft and gentle that they can sing the whole night without getting tired."[29] He further says, "The Mizo in the early period were very close to nature and that music was the tune of their life."[30]

Drum

Drum (*Khuang*) is one of the Mizo indigenous musical instruments from the olden days. It played a very significant role in the social and religious life. It is a must on all occasions. Mangkhosat Kipgen writes, "it was indispensable for singing and dancing around the beer pot in their homes, during festival and feasts of various types. It is significant that *Khuangchawi*, the feast that conferred the performer with the coveted *thangchhuah* title, derived its name from *Khuang*, the *Zo* term for drum."[31]

As far as the history of Mizo is concerned it is commonly concluded that the Mizo ancestors started using drum as early as when they started singing and composing songs. Lianhmingthanga believes that Mizo received drum from the Chinese civilization through cultural diffusion. The process of that cultural diffusion might have passed through the Burmese with whom the Mizo had a close cultural contact, which took place from the middle of the 9th century AD until the end of pagan at the close of 13th century AD.[32] According to R. L. Thanmawia, *Khuang* is the only Mizo traditional musical instrument that is popularly used in the 20th and 21st centuries.[33] Therefore, *Khuang* is important in the Mizo society. There is one popular saying, "*Khuang lova chai ang*" which means "festival without drum." This shows that for the Mizo without drum the life of the Mizo was incomplete.

Public Feasts

One of the characteristics of the traditional festivals was the public feasts, which had connected both social and religious practices. In the old days, the wealthy families would give a series of public feasts, which they believed would help them to reach *Pialral* (village for the dead). As festivals were celebrated with gaiety and enjoyable community feasting, the people look forward to the advent festivals with great eagerness.

Significance of the Festivals

The following discussion tries to give some of the importance of festivals in the life of the Mizo before the coming of Christianity.

Festivals Related to Mizo Economy

As discussed earlier, the economic life of the Mizo was based on agriculture, in the form of *jhumming*. The *Chapchar Kut* was observed after completing cutting the jungle, the *Mim Kut* was celebrated at the time of harvest of maize and other vegetables, and the *Pawl Kut* was celebrated after the annual harvests of the main food grain. Therefore, the festivals of the Mizo revolve around the *jhumming* and were closely connected with agricultural practices. All the three main festivals are in one way or the other associated with their economic. With plenty of grain in their ban, and all the labours of the year over, the villagers would snatch a rest and enjoy the fruits of their labour.

Festivals Related to Community

One Indian scholar, S. N. Singh came out his finding the importance of festival in the Mizo society. He writes, "The festivals have promoted community feeling and have helped in influencing the attitude of the Mizo. Every festival is accompanied with dance and music, which is the symbol of their love and fellow feeling. The community feasts and festivals have widened the boundary of community life."[34] In the words of E. J. Thomas, the significance of the festivals in the Mizo social can be read as, "it served to strengthen community solidarity."[35] People eagerly look forward to *Kut* because all sections of the society, whether poor or rich, enjoyed themselves on such occasions. There was no distinction between the rich and the poor during the festivals. Moreover, in these festivals the poor benefited from the richer people who contributed rice-beer and feasts. Therefore, according to M. Lalmuanzuala, the festivals are the "centre of the Mizo culture."[36]

Festivals Promoted Unity and Integrity

To mention some of the celebration, like dating and consuming of rice-beer in the feast, wearing of traditional dress, dancing in several times, etc., were all done in such a manner as the social life of the community. Co-operation of many members symbolized social unity and integrity. Successful completion of festivals, every year, indicated the unified strengthen and stability of the community. Festivals, therefore, gave the people their social traditions and customary responsibilities and attachment.

Function of the Festivals

In the Mizo society, the village Chief played an important role. He was the sole authority of the land. In fact, the appointments of the date for festivals were mostly the responsibility of the Chief and elders. People joined hands with them as faithful loyalists. Only the designated persons like the *Sadawt* can perform the important religious rites. The public can participate in the dance. Even then people were happy to participate in the festivals as a sign of honour to their rulers and also to strengthen their adherence to traditional and culture. Thus, the symbol of political unity was manifested right from the time of preparation till the end of the festivals celebration.

Festivals and Religious Beliefs

Whether or not the festivals were related to the Mizo traditional religion is a significant question. There is no an agreement among the writers. Some writers like D. Baveja,[37] E. J. Thomas, J. V. Hluna[38] and James Dokhuma support that the Mizo traditional festivals were related to the religious beliefs. According to them the festivals played an important role in the religious life of the Mizo. Generally, the Mizo are very superstitious people, which made them to connect the social events to their religious beliefs. Therefore, social beliefs were deeply attached to their religious beliefs, too.[39]

On the other hand, there are some writers namely K. Zawla, R. L. Thanmawia and Lalthangfala Sailo[40] who believe that the relationship of the Mizo traditional festivals and the religious beliefs was more social than religious. According to them, these traditional festivals were more social than religious in character. Indian writer K. P. Nath also supports the above discussion by saying, "These festivals were more social than religious in their characters."[41] Even one of the early missionaries in North Mizoram, J. M. Lloyd remarks, "Although these festivals were not strictly religious festivals a kind of religious aura attached to them and there were many taboos to be observed, and many semi-sacred rites and customs to be performed."[42]

Therefore, when we study the life of the Mizo in the old days, we see that their religious ideas or beliefs system affected their social, economic and political life. Hence, it is difficult to differentiate the social life from the religious life.

People could express the remembrance of their ancestors and honour them by offering foods, vegetables and others at the time of *Mim Kut*. Therefore, this act symbolized the role of the festival in projecting a sense of continuing relationship with the ancestors, which is one of the main features of the Mizo traditional beliefs.

In the celebration of the festivals, sacred person like *Sadawt* or priest was also involved. As noted earlier, the *Sadawt* performed religious rites in the celebration of *Chapchar Kut* and *Pawl Kut* festivals. Hence, only the designated persons of the clans act as facilitators of sacrifices or some other religious rites.

Concluding Remarks

From the above discussion we may said that the life of the Mizo in the old days was full of celebrations. They celebrated three main festivals, *Chapchar Kut*, *Mim Kut* and *Pawl Kut* with gaiety and merriment in all villages. These three main festivals were became very important cultural traditions in the Mizo society. In these festivals, drinking of rice-beer, singing and dancing and public feasts were the main public entertainment.

End Notes

1 K. Zawla, *Mizo Pi Pute leh An Thlahte Chanchin*, revised and enlarged (Aizawl: The Author, 1993), 61. Hereafter cited as Zawla, *Mizo Pi Pute leh An Thlahte Chanchin*.

2 B. Lalthangliana, *Pi Pu Chhuahtlang* (*Studies in Mizo Culture and Folktales*) (Aizaw: Hrangbana College, 1998), 85.

3 C. Lalbiaknema, *Kan Chenna Mizoram* (Aizawl: Synod Literature and Publication Board, 1995), 36.

4 Zawla, *Mizo Pi Pute leh An Thlahte Chanchin*, 53.

5 James Dokhuma, *Hmanlai Mizo Kalphung* (Aizawl: J. D. Press Publication, 1992), 77. Hereafter cited as Dokhuma, *Hmanlai Mizo Kalphung*.

6 R. L. Thanzawna, "The Origin of Chapchar Kut," in *Chapchar Kut Souvenir* (Aizawl: Chapchar Kut Organizing Committee, 2003), 43.

7 Ibid., 44.

8 B. Lalthangliana, *India, Burma leh Bangladesh-a Mizo Chanchin* (Aizawl: Remkungi, 2001), 308. Hereafter cited as Lalthangliana, *India, Burma leh Bangladesh-a Mizo Chanchin*.

9 Sangkima, *Mizos: Society and Social Change 1890-1947*, 62. (italic mines).

10 Thingpui tam: "to die simultaneously as certain forests trees do in large numbers periodically. The intervals between, however, are so long that even old men only remember having heard tell of the last occasion when such a thing occurred." See Lorrain, *Dictionary of the Lushai Language*, 467.

11 Sangkima, *Mizos: Society and Social Change 1890-1947*, 63.

12 Sangkima, *Mizos: Society and Social Change 1890-1947*, 63; Shakespear, *The Lusei Kuki Clan*, 87; Parry, *Lushai Customs and Ceremonies*, 91, 92.

13 C. G. Varghese and R. L. Thanzawna, *A History of the Mizos*, vol. I (New Delhi: Vikas Publishing House Pvt. Ltd., 1997), 23.

14 Vawkpa Sutnghak: a hog, which has been dedicated and set apart for a sacrificial to one's *sakhua*. To sell such a pig is considered *thianglo* and likely to bring about death. See Lorrain, *Dictionary of the Lushai Language*, 547.

15 C. Lianthanga, *Hmanlai Mizo Nun* (Aizawl: Mizoram Publication Board, 1999), 112. Hereafter cited as Liangthanga, *Hmanlai Mizo Nun*.

16 Chhawnghnawt: 'the name of a children's and young people's feast held during the *Chapchar Kut* and *Pawl Kut* festivals, either in the village square or near the memorial platforms of the departed just outside the village. A prominent feature of this feast is the way it is eaten. The Children and young people stuff the boiled rice, hard-boiled eggs and meat into one another's mouths amidst much merriment. While others wail as they remember the departed.' See Lorrain, *Dictionary of the Lushai Language*, 76.

17 Animesh Ray, *Mizoram* (New Delhi: National Book Trust, 1993), 131.

18 Hrilh: To solemnize by abstaining from going to the jhum.

19 V. L. Siama, *Mizo History*, re-print (Aizawl: Lengchhawn Press, 1991), 85. Hereafter cited as Siama, *Mizo History*.

20 Lianthanga, *Hmanlai Mizo Nun*, 121.

21 Ar mit rawh: The name of a ceremony by which boys or girls maternal grandfather or uncle, or anyone acting as such, publicly proclaims his relationship to him or her. Providing a fowl, pig, or other animal for a feast in the boy's or girl's home does this. When performed by a relative this is really a sacrifice on behalf of the boy or girl. See Lorrain, *Dictionary of the Lushai Language*, 13.

22 Zawla, *Mizo Pi Pute leh An Thlahte Chanchin*, 52.

23 Dokhuma, *Hmanlai Mizo Kalphung*, 87; Lalthangliana, *India, Burma leh Bangladesh-a Mizo Chanchin*, 309.

24 *Zu in Mizo Society (Past and Present)* (Aizawl: Senior Research Officer, Tribal Research Institute, 1983), 1.

25 Ibid., 43.

26 Lalthangliana, *India, Burma leh Bangladesh-a Mizo Chanchin*, 311.

27 Darchhawna, "Development and spread of Gospel Songs in Mizoram," *Chapchar Kut Souvenir* (Aizawl: Chapchar Kut Organizing Committee, 2003), 27.

28 Zatluanga, *Mizo Chanchin* (aizawl: n.p., 1996), 33, 34.

29 R. L. Thanmawia, "Heritage of the Mizo Traditional Music (An overview)," *Chapchar Kut Souvenir* (Aizawl: Chapchar Kut Organizing Committee, 2003), 40. Hereafter cited as Thanmawia, "Heritage of the Mizo Traditional Music."

30 Ibid.

31 Kipgen, *Christianity and Mizo Culture*, 271.

32 Lianhmingthanga, *Material Culture of the Mizo* (Calcutta: Firma KLM Private Limited, 1998), 30.

33 Thanmawia, "*Heritage of the Mizo Traditional Music*," 36.

34 S. N. Singh, *Mizoram: Historical, Geographical, Social, Economic, Political and Administrative* (New Delhi: Mittal Publication, 1994), 60, 61.

35 E. J. Thomas, *Mizo: Bamboo Hills Murmur Change* (New Delhi: Intellectual Publishing House, 1993), 7.

36 M. Lalmanzuala, *Zoram Kalsiam-* 2 (Aizawl: Sapthlengliana, 1999), 58, 59.

37 D. Baveja, *The Land where the Bamboo Flowers* (Guwahati: Publication Board, 1970), 36.

38 J. V. Hluna, "Education in Mizoram with Special Reference to the Role of the Missions" (Ph. D. Dissertation, Gauhati Univeristy, 1985), 28, 29. Hereafter cited as Hluna, "Education in Mizoram…"

39 Lalnghakthuami, "A Theological Examination of the Selected Mizo Festivals (Chapchar Kut, Mim Kut and Pawl Kut): Towards a Theology of Mizo Culture" (M. Th. Thesis, Senate of Serampore College, 1995), 60.

40 Lalthangfala Sailo, "Chapchar Kut," *Chapchar Kut Souvenir* (Aizawl: Chapchar Kut Organizing Committee, 2003), 6.

41 K. P. Nath, "Mizo Value, Beliefs and Practices Vis-à-vis Christianity," Studies on the Minority Nationalities of Northeast India- The Mizo Seminar paper (Aizawl: Romesh Buragohain, 1992), 39.

42 Lloyd, *History of the Church in Mizoram*, 11.

Chapter 3

Introduction of Christianity in Mizoram

Mizoram was opened to the Gospel and the salvation of Jesus Christ through various means. The British Government annexed the land in 1885 and made the British reign in Mizoram. Christianity also followed the British flag. Christian missionaries began their operations in the territory of present day Mizoram in 1891. During the last decade of the nineteenth century, Protestant missionary work was started in Mizoram and later became important centre of the Christian movement.[1] This portion deals with a brief history of the missionary societies from the West.

The Forerunner

The earliest record of the Christian contact with the Mizo can be traced back to the visit made by Rev. William Williams, the Welsh Presbyterian missionary working at Shella in the Khasi Hills on March 15, 1891.[2] J. M. Lloyd quoted the record of his visit and his observation about the religio-cultural life of the Mizo. He quotes, "we made an attempt to tell them about God. They all said that God was good. They call God *Khuavang* and he makes his home high above. *Khua* means 'village' and '*veng*' is guard. Their language is most musical and its intonation remarkably beautiful. It falls with tender melody upon the ear. I believe that it will be like Welsh, a good pulpit language."[3] William Williams was very much attracted by the Mizo and he wrote to the Mission headquarters in Liverpool to undertake Mizoram for its mission field. He himself volunteered to be missionary in Mizoram. He left Aizawl on April 11, 1891. Although, he stayed for a short period of time only, he was the first missionary who "first sound the name of Jesus" to the Mizo and the first one who brought to light the prospect of founding a new mission field for the Welsh Presbyterian Church.[4] After five years of his recommendation, the Welsh Mission formally adopted Mizoram as its mission field.

Mission Societies

The Arthington Aborigines Mission

The Arthington Aborigines Mission[5] established its mission field in the Lushai Hills. The mission waited at silchar for permission to enter Mizoram from the Government in 1893. On January 11, 1894 the two missionaries of this mission, J. H. Lorrain (known as Pu Buanga) and F. W. Savidge (known as Sap Upa) entered Mizoram. The mission had some unusual rules, "one was that the missionaries should be unmarried. Another was that they should proclaim the Gospel and then move on to others fields, leaving the business of church organization to others."[6] Lorrain and Savidge stayed for four years in Mizoram. Their contributions during these four years were remarkable. They laid the foundation for the future of Christian missions. They devoted themselves to learning and reduce the language into written form using the Roman scripts. Nag observes, "They were the first who taught a number of Mizo how to read and write."[7] They completed the translation of the *Gospels of Luke* and *John*, and *the Acts of the Apostles* in Mizo language. Mizo had the whole New Testament translation in their own language in May 1916, and a revised edition was available in 1923. They wrote hymns, a catechism, a simple primer, a grammar, and produced a dictionary of seven thousand words.[8] Lorrain also composed *A*

Grammar and Dictionary of Lushai Language, which was published by the Government of Assam in 1898. Lorrain and Savidge were willing to sacrifice their church identity to remain in the region. They requested the Welsh Mission to accept them as its evangelists, but the Welsh mission could not accept them.[9] Therefore, Lorrain and Savidge left Mizoram at the end of 1897. Lalsangkima Pachuau remarks, "The Arthington Mission's work in Mizoram within a short period of time was unforgettable for the Mizo."[10] After they left Mizoram they work among the Abor and Miri tribes of the present day Arunachal Pradesh. After some years they came back to the southern part of Mizoram as missionaries of the Baptist Missionary Society.

Welsh Calvinistic Methodist Mission

The first missionary of the Welsh Calvinistic Methodist Mission (later known as Welsh Presbyterian Mission) D. E. Jones accompanied by T. J. Jones and a Khasi Christian teacher, Rai Bhajur and his wife, arrived in Aizawl on August 31, 1897. Rai Bahajur gave up his job as Sub-Inspector of Schools in the Khasi Hills in order to serve as an evangelist in Mizoram. He remained with Jones until another Welsh missionary arrived at the end of the following year. Jones and Bhajur stayed with Lorrain and Savidge four four months. They benefited greatly from the experience and teaching of Pu Buanga and Sap Upa, who were to help them for four months. In the next year, Edwin Rowlands joined them. *The Report of the Lushai Hills 1901-1902* clearly mentioned that the Welsh Missionary work was divided into four branches, namely education, preaching, medical, and literature.[11] After the Baptist Mission came into contact with the Southern portion of the Lushai Hills in 1903, the Welsh Mission concentrated only in the North Lushai Hills. The mission established schools, a theological school, hospital, etc. Within 71 years of Welsh Mission work, there were altogether 54 Welsh missionaries including their wives.[12] The Presbyterian Church became the largest denomination. The Welsh mission contributed much to the social improvement of the Mizo society by providing primary education. They also contributed to the Mizo social change and development through their medical work. Chatterjee observes;

> Members of the Welsh Mission did their best in their capacities to improve the lot of the Lushai people. They were more interested in charitable works than that of proselytizing... The missionary teachers, medical men and nurses were all dedicated persons. A large number of European ladies of the Welsh Mission helped in dignifying the missionary enterprise. In those days when the life in the Lushai country was not at all secure those dedicated sisters of the Church undaunted marched from one to the other hills with the purpose of serving humanity.[13]

Baptist Missionary Society

In 1901 one of the missionaries of the British Baptist Missionary Society (BMS) in Chittagong, George Hughes, urgently appealed to his mission headquarters to take the southern part of the Lushai hills.[14] The BMS requested the Welsh mission "to transfer the southern portion of the Lushai Hills to their care."[15] Though D. E. Jones and Edwin Rowland both Welsh Missionaries rejected the plan, the Welsh Mission Board handed over the southern portion to the BMS on the ground that, "the BMS was a larger and wealthier organization with more manpower to deploy."[16] J. H. Lorrain and F. W. Savidge arrived Lunglei on March 13, 1903 as the Baptist Missionary Society missionaries.[17] During the 55 years of the Baptist Missionary Society's work in the South Mizoram, 23 missionaries had served in the field.[18] The Baptist Church became the second largest denomination next to the Presbyterian Church. The contribution of the Baptist Missionary Society may not be less than the Welsh Mission in the North.

Lakher Pioneer Mission

Another important mission work was started in the most southern part of Mizoram in 1907. When one of the students of a Lakher youth in the Baptist Mission School in Lunglei accepted Christ, J. H. Lorrain, Baptist Missionary at Lunglei requested his brother, Reginald A. Lorrain to come and start mission work among the

Lakher. R. A. Lorrain and his wife were arrived Serkawr in 1907 and started the Lakher Pioneer Mission in the South Mizoram. Within five years, R. A. Lorrain reduced the language to writing and produced a dictionary, a hymn book, and translated the Gospel of John.[19]

The above discussion shows that three Missionary Societies worked together in Mizoram. These Missionary Societies contributed much to the Mizo socio-cultural change. Their sincere efforts won the heart of the people to God. Hence, it is clear that Christianity brought by the Christian missionaries of these societies played a vital role in the socio-cultural change among the Mizo. Therefore, we can rightly point out that Christianity was the primary agent of change in Mizoram.

Other Denominations

The Government of India restricted the entry of non-recognised missionary societies or organization with the introduction of The Memoranda of 1919.[20] The Government used the Memoranda, "to prevent missionaries, especially non-British missionaries, from giving support to Indian nationalists."[21] Memorandum 'C' stated that members of any non-recognised society or organization must obtain a permit from the Government of India.[22] Likewise, the Hills Officers' Conference held at Shillong on July 21, 1937 discussed the relationship between officials and missions working in the areas. The conference felt that the entry of non-recognised missionary societies or organization in the Hills areas should be restricted. The Conference resolves:

> Since there are Missions in every Hill district it is undesirable that any others should be allowed in.[23]

The Government of Assam also restricted the entry of missionary organizations either to start fresh activities or to operate missions in the Hills.[24] In Mizoram, the Welsh Presbyterian Mission, London Baptist Mission, Lakher Pioneer Mission, Salvation Army, Roman Catholic and Seventh Day Adventist were the recognised missions by the Government till 1949.[25] With the passage of time other Christian missions of different denominations and Christian groups, and other indigenous churches also made their way into Mizoram during the twentieth century. While the number of missionaries stationed in this region was always small, they were amazingly successful in their work.

Concluding Remarks

Christianity has continued to make gains since Indian independence, even after foreign missionaries were excluded. Thus by 2001, there were 772,809 Christians, accounting for 87.0% of the total population.[26] We see that in a period of one hundred years, the inhabitants of Mizoram have overwhelmingly adopted Christianity, and it has become a Christian state. Some observation of the rapid growth of Christianity in Mizoram can be highlighted. Kipgen observed that within sixty years of its introduction, all the Mizo have became Christian and have put old religious practices behind them.[27] Downs also believes that Mizoram is the "area in which Christianity grew most rapidly at the beginning of the twentieth century."[28] Two lady missionaries who worked in South Mizoram, Edith M. Chapman and M. Clark also describe that "the response of the people to Christian teaching was very rapid, and the church grew and developed with remarkable speed."[29] Lloyd accordingly observes the growth of the Church in Mizoram, by claiming it to be, "unprecedented in any other parts of Southern Asia."[30] Commenting on the work done by the missionaries in Mizoram Suhas Chatterjee in his study *Mizoram under the British Rule*, writes, "The history of missionary enterprise in the Lushai Hills is indeed glorious. It is no exaggeration to state that the missionaries were the real torchbearers of civilization among the ignorant Lushai population."[31] The above observation indicates that the Gospel seed was sown in Mizoram and multiplied with a large number of fruits.

End Notes

1 Frederick S. Downs, *Christianity in North East India* (Delhi: ISPCK, 1983), 117. Hereafter cited as Downs, *Christianity in North East India*.

2 K. Thanzauva, comp., *Reports of the Foreign Mission of the Presbyterian Church of Wales on Mizoram 1894-1957* (Aizawl: The Synod Literature and Publication Board, 1997), 1. Hereafter cited as Thanzauva, *RFMPCWM.*

3 Lloyd, *History of the Church in Mizoram*, 21.

4 Saiaithanga, *Mizo Kohhran Chanchin*, 3rd print (Aizawl: The Mizo Theological Literature Committee, 1993), 10.

5 Arthington Aborigines Mission: The founder of Arthington Aborigines Mission, Robert Arthington (1823-1900) was a wealthy person of Leeds, England. He believed in the urgent priority of pioneer evangelism, and much of his giving was conditioned upon the willingness of missionary societies to embark as new projects in virgin territory. The Arthington Aborigines Mission established in 1889, pioneered work in Mizoram, and laid the foundations for the extraordinary success of the Welsh Presbyterian Church and Baptist Missionary Society in this part of North East India.

6 Downs, *Christianity in North East India*, 188.

7 Chitta Ranjan Nag, *The Mizo Society in Transition* (New Delhi: Vikash Publishing House Pvt. Ltd., 1993), 122.

8 M. Eleanor Bowser, *Light on the Lushai Hills: The Story of a Dream that Come True* (London: The Carey Press, n.d.), 10.

9 Hminga, *The Life and Witness of the Churches in Mizoram*, 50-51.

10 Lalsangkima Pachuau, *Robert Arthington-a leh a Ramthar Rawngbawlna Chanchin* (Robert Arthington and His Foreign Missions) (Aizawl: Synod Publication Board, 1994), 28.

11 K. Thanzauva, *RFMPRCWM*, 11.

12 Lalkhawliana and C. Sangzuala, ed., *Mizoram Gospel Centennial Jubilee-1994* (Aizawl: The Gospel Centenary Sub-Committee on Souvenir for and on behalf of the Mizoram Presbyterian Church Synod, n.d), 53-54.

13 Suhas Chatterjee, *Mizoram under the British Rule* (New Delhi: Mittal Publication, 1985), 200-201. Hereafter cited as Chatterjee, *Mizoram under the British.*

14 Lloyd, *History of the Church*, 74.

15 Donna Strom, *Wind through the Bamboo: The Story of Transformed Mizo*, reprint (Madras: Evangelical Literature Service, 1991), 33. Hereafter cited as Strom, *Wind Through the Bamboo.*

16 Lloyd, *History of the Church*, 75.

17 H. W. Carter, *Chhim Bial Kohhran Chanchin* (Serkawn: Rev. H. W. Carter, 1945), 50.

18 Hminga, *The Life and Witness of the Churches in Mizoram*, 242.

19 Reginald A. Lorrain, *Five Years in Unknown Jungles* (London: Lakher Pioneer Mission, 1912), 269.

20 Critical analysis of the Memoranda was carried out by D. Arthur Jeyakumar, *Christians and the National Movement, The Memoranda of 1919 and the National Movement with Special reference to Protestant Christians in Tamil Nadu:*

1919-1939 (Calcutta: Punthi Pustak, 1999). Hereftaer cited as Jeyakumar, *The Memoranda.*

21 Jeyakumar, *The Memoranda*, 162.

22 Jeyakumar, *The Memoranda*, 177.

23 Resolution No. 4 in the Proceeding of the Hills Officers' Conference held at Shillong on July 21, 1937.

24 N. K. Rustomji, Adviser to the H. E. the Governor of Assam for Excluded Areas and States Letter D. O. No. 59/48/C-247-245, Shillong, the 17th February, 1949 to the Superintendent, Lushai Hills.

25 L. L. Peters, Superintendent, Lushai Hills Letter D. O. No. 15597/C, Aijal 23-2-1949 to N. K. Rustomji, Adviser to H. E. the Governor of Assam for Excluded Areas and States, Shillong.

26 Census 2001, xxix.

27 Kipgen, *Christianity and Mizo Culture*, 210.

28 Downs, *Christianity in NEI*, 118.

29 Eddith M. Chapman and M. Clark, *Mizo Miracle* (Madras: The Christian Literature Society, 1968), 86. Hereafter cited as Chapman and Clark, *Mizo Miracle.*

30 Lloyd, "Presbyterian," 3.

31 Chatterjee, *Mizoram under the British*, 201.

Chapter 4

Interaction Between Christianity and Mizo Cultural Practices

This chapter is to examine the interaction between Christianity and the Mizo traditional culture. It is an important subject to study because Christianity brought many cultural changes among the Mizo. The coming of Christianity through the Christian missionaries made drastic change in the life of the Mizo.

Encounter Between Christianity and Mizo Culture

Richard Neihbur defines culture as,

> The total process of human activity and the total result of such activity, which comprises language, habit, ideas, belief, custom, social organization, inherited artifacts, technical process, and values. On other words, total "social heritage."[1]

Yeow Choo Lak[2] understands "culture covers everything in life (human) and is learnt afresh by each generation in the social activities (home or village gatherings, initiation rites, etc.,)."[3]

Therefore, the culture of a group of people can be understood in terms of the commonness in conception and practices through which people are being socialized accordingly.[4] Lalsangkima Pachuau also defines culture as "common behavior shared by a community."[5] Therefore, from the above discussion, it is clear that culture should be understood in term of the community life of the people. Then, when we speak of the Mizo culture, we mean that the whole life of the Mizo community whether before or after Christian present in Mizoram. The following discussion will deal with the encounter between Christianity and Mizo traditional culture.

Missionary Attitude towards Mizo Culture

Most of the Mizo history writers believed that the missionaries were responsible for the cultural change among the Mizo. N. E. Parry felt that the missionaries were destroying some of the excellent customs of the Lushai. He observes:

> When mission work was first started among the Lusheis it was carried on largely by the light of nature, without training and without knowledge of customs of the people. This led to the condemnation of heathen and useless of some most excellent customs, which no one who had studies them could have failed to wish to preserve....Through lack of knowledge, therefore, excellent customs which would have great strengthened the Church, while at the same time keeping it Lushei and adverting denationalization, were left unused, and actually discouraged.[6]

The above quotation shows that it is harmful to do missionary work to the heathen people without having knowledge of their customs. When the Christian missionaries came into Mizoram from foreign countries, their main aim was to preach the Gospel and to proselytize the native to Christianity. Most of the missionaries came without any knowledge of the Mizo. They brought with them the western culture and theology, which they imposed upon the native affecting, changes in their social and religious customs. These made a lot of changes among the Mizo to their social-customs. Lalsawma clearly described missionaries' attitude to the Mizo culture specially connected to the traditional festivals. According to him, missionaries restricted Christians from:[7]

1) Joining or taking part in *Chawng* feast and festival,
2) drinking any kind of rice-beer,
3) singing the Mizo traditional songs and its tune,
4) taking part in traditional dances,
5) participating in the sacrifices.

One of the main causes for change in the Mizo society was the introduction of education. Lalrimawia believes that the introduction of education became the factor for the gradual growth of different opinion between the British administrator and the missionaries in respect of the Mizo indigenous practices. He notes,

> The administrators were in favour of retaining many of the indigenous practices and institution such as drinking, dancing, slavery, *Zawlbuk* (bachelor dormitory), whereas the missionaries did not allow the Lushai converts to have any connection with them. Rather they enforced strict taboo on drinking, indigenous festivals, *Zawlbuk*, and a few other institutions which has some of connections in one way or other with their old religion.[8]

McCall also points out that the changes, which took place among the Lushai villagers, were greatly due to the missionary fervor. He further says, "The changes they have wrought have been often spectator, necessarily involving attack on tradition. It is, however, one thing to eradicate and another to build up securely."[9] Hrangkhuma Fanai also agrees with the other writers. According to him, though the missionaries destroyed much of the Mizo life, they also built much. He notes, "The missionaries exercised some degree of cultural imposition, perhaps due to a failure to distinguish between culture and gospel."[10]

On the other hand, according to E, Chapman and M. Clark, the goal set by the pioneer missionaries was the establishment of the Mizo church. The missionaries hoped to "retain all that is good in

Mizo life while following on to what is better."[11] Some Mizo leaders who were influenced by the missionaries did not see a negative attitude towards the Mizo culture by the missionaries. Chalhnuna insists that the missionaries did not have any opposition to the Mizo culture.[12]

The above discussion shows that there are two groups of Mizo history writers having different opinions on the missionaries' attitude toward Mizo culture. The first group like the British administrators McCall, N. E. Parry and other blamed that the missionaries destroyed many elements of the Mizo culture. The second groups mostly missionaries themselves and the missionary influenced writers claimed that the missionaries had no negative attitude. If we study carefully, we may say that the attitude of missionaries towards Mizo culture had both positive and negative influence.

Christianity and Traditional Beliefs

With the advent of the Christian gospel, the interaction between Christianity and Mizo religious practices is noticeable. Some writers like Laltluangliana Khiangte, Lalnghinglova, and others observe that Christianity and Mizo traditional belief were almost the same, like their belief of God, the concept of life after death, and the demon position. Thus, according to Lalnghinglova, "the gift of Christianity was only Jesus Christ and Christianity."[13] As we have discussed under the religious life of the people in the previous chapter, the Mizo acknowledge one supreme and benevolent god called *Pathian*. With the spread of Christianity, "belief in *Pathian* continued with a new connotation as God of Christianity."[14] Kipgen also writes,

> Formerly *Pathian* was viewed as far removed and unconcerned with human affairs. However, in the course of time it began to be believed that he did in fact reveal himself known to the people as an essentially paternal figure who blessed his people. By the time Christianity was introduced this understanding of a revealed and benevolent religion as practiced by the Lusei clan was

well on its way to becoming the religious understanding of all the Zo people in Mizoram.[15]

In the old traditional practices, the sacrifices offers to demons and evil spirits were the most central concept of worship in sacrifice. Sacrifices to the evil spirits were to appease them for healing from sickness. In the old days, there was no certainty of cure for disease. On the other hand, in the words of McCall, when Christianity was introduced, "the Christian, many believe, can secure certainty of salvation by regular attendance at the church and a sincere confession of sins. Sacrifices and feasts are no longer a necessity. Medicine is a cheap and more certain cause for disease than the costly sacrifices of old."[16] Hence, the Mizo no longer practicised sacrifices to the evil spirits after they became Christian.

The early Mizo believed that after death their soul went to *Pialral.* To go to *Pialral* one had to achieve the status of *Thangchhuah.* There are two kind of *Thangchhuah*, namely *Ram Lama Thangchhuah* (killing a certain number of different animals) and *In lama Thangchhuah* (giving a certain number of public feasts). If one had achieved one of the *Thangchhuah*, he would go to *Pialral.* Moreover, "*Pialral* in old Lushai thought was the destiny of the skilful, powerful and the rich. But after becoming Christian, *Pialral* has come to mean 'heaven' or 'paradise', the home of the redeemed."[17] C. L. Hminga also observes, "Christianity offered them at just that time a new and better way to get paradise... The Mizo conception of '*Pialral*' was transformed by the Christian conception of 'heaven.' Thus, Christianity has transformed the Mizo eschatology also."[18]

Therefore, the above discussion shows that the Mizo traditional beliefs had pave the way for the rapid spread of Christianity in Mizoram. As most of the Mizo religious practices and teaching of Christianity are almost the same, it is not difficult for the Mizo to accept Christianity for their religion.

Mizo Christians Attitude towards Traditional Festivals

In the previous chapter, we have already discussed in detailed the origin of the Mizo traditional festivals and its elements. We have also mentioned about the religious significance of the festivals. As we have mentioned there, the three main festivals, *Chapchar Kut*, *Mim Kut* and *Pawl Kut*, were celebrated with feasts and dance. The Mizo celebrated these festivals with great gaiety and fervor. When Christianity came into Mizoram, the early converts and missionaries mostly felt that the Mizo traditional festivals were connected with animistic religious practices. Therefore, the first Mizo Presbytery (now Synod) meeting in 1910 resoled that Christians should refrain from unchristian practices of *Kawngpui Siam* and *Fano Dawi* in Mizo culture.[19] Christians were also forbidden to participate in the festivals and indulge in the drinking and merry-making celebrations.

Christianity has brought a tremendous change in perception of traditional Mizo festivals. With the introduction of Christianity these festivals "have lost their significance and are not observed any more as they were once observed with great gaiety, fervor and fanfare."[20] When the church was born, it was uncompromising and discipline was strict.[21] Therefore, the church became very strict on some of the elements of the traditional festivals. The following discussion will try to deal with the attitudes of the missionaries and the early Mizo Christian to the traditional festivals.

Drinking of Zu

We had discussed the importance of *zu* (rice-beer) in the pre-Christian Mizo society especially at the time of festivals. Here, we need not give any detail on the importance of *zu* in the celebration of festivals. Instead, we try to study how and why the missionaries and the church condemned *zu* drinking.

When Christianity came into Mizoram, "*zu* drinking was condemned by the missionaries from the very beginning, and those who wanted to become Christians had to give up."[22] The giving up of *zu* means, "he testifies that he was giving up the practices of that religion."[23] Zairema notes, "If you as much as lick your fingers dipped in rice-beer, you are liable to excommunication."[24] Those who were against these rules were removed from the church's membership. In his research K. Lalrinmawia states that there are three important factors for the missionaries to build negative attitude towards drinking rice-beer. The following are the factors:[25]

(1) they regarded the Mizos' use of *Zu* as excessive and problematic;
(2) they saw *Zu* as inseparable from the religion of the Mizos; and
(3) some of the missionaries were total abstainers, with a strong dislike for alcoholic drinkers. The *Zu* was rejected and unaccepted by the Churches, yet it still.

Lalnghakthuami discussed the reason why Christians gave up of drinking rice-beer. She writes, "Festivals, dances and songs were closely attached with drinking of rice-beer and meat; therefore, the old people could not perform festival without rice-beer, dance and song. For them, it would be re-establishment of rice-beer in the society."[26] C. L. Hminga also believes that the excessive drinking during these festivals was the reason that the early Mizo Christians insisted on total abstinence from drinking.[27] The missionary did not allow the Mizo converts to have any connection with the old life. Rather they enforced strict taboo on drinking, local festivals, dancing and singing, though some of these were really worth practicing.[28]

On the other hand, the condemnation of rice-beer drinking has given a wide impetus to tea drinking. "But, this in turn has also led to an increase in dyspepsia and bowel complaints, as much of the tea drinking is not of the best, and the evil practices soon arose stewing the tea rather than infusing the tea with boiling water," says McCall.[29] In his personal letter to Peter, Shakespear expressed his dislike of the Padres condemnation of *zu*, he writes.

> The most wonderful to me is that the Padres have got Lushais to give up *Zu*. That seems to me really a miracle. Of course I don't entirely approve. The Lushais in my day were not drunkards. They liked an occasional bust and were none the worse for it, because *Zu* is a most healthy drink, and I think a man who can drink in moderation is a fined fellow than one who never touches *Zu*.[30]

Re-introduction of Indigenous Drum

"The early Mizo Christian community did not use the drum during the first two decades of its history. Because of its association with the traditional festivals and drinking bouts, the missionaries and the early Mizo Christians precluded the drum from the church," says Lalsangkima Pachuau.[31] The above quotation clearly mentioned that the missionaries and the early church attitude to the element of the Mizo traditional festivals. The introduction of drum in the Christian church has seen through the revival movement.

However, the date of the first introduction of a drum in the Christian church is still debated. Some writers like Liangkhaia,[32] Saiaithanga,[33] C. L. Hminga[34] and V. L. Siama[35] regarded that the drum was introduced during the third Revival in 1919. Lalsawm, however, placed for drum introduction during the Second Revival in 1913.[36] Z. T. Sangkhuma argued that the church in Nisapui village was the first to use drum in the church.[37] Mizo Feminist theologian, Lalrinawm Ralte explains the importance of the introduction of drum in the church, she writes.

> The use of drum in the revival movement was the first manifestation of indigenization within the [Mizo] Christian community. The traditional musical gifts were a result of the encounter with Christianity in the form of ecstatic revivals at the deepest levels of Mizo culture. It was this aspect of Mizo culture that contributed to the continuance of revivalism among Christians.[38]

On the other hand, the missionaries had different opinion on the introduction of drum in the church. According to Lalsangkima, "the absence of the drum in the churches at the two mission centers of the Baptists and the Presbyterians appears to indicate the missionaries' negative attitude toward this distinctive worship instrument."[39] Llyod also clearly highlighted missionaries' attitude to the introduction of drum in the church in his book *History of the Church in Mizoram*. He writes,

> Whether the uncontrolled use of the drum at this time was an advantage or not is still a moot and arguable point, particularly as the use of it was often in very unreliable hands. The drummer was as a rule self-appointed, but controlled a very potent instrument. The presence of the

> drum affected meetings profoundly and has a mesmeric influence on many. It induced and controlled the church service in 1919 more than in any previous revival. The repetitive singing of the same hymn was largely though not together due to the use of drum. This trouble many for they feared that hymn-singing was ousting prayer, scripture reading and preaching, or at least pushing them into the background. The drum appeared to dictate to the congregation and even to the Holy Spirit.[40]

Here, we see clearly the negative attitude of the missionaries in the re-introduction of Mizo indigenous drum in the church. Lloyd pointed out four points in which the church cannot accept the introduction of drum 1) the drummers are self-appointed, 2) had enticing influence on the people, 3) this trouble many, and 4) dictated the congregation and even the Holy Spirit. Whether the statements are true or not is debatable. It may not be true to say that the drum disturbed the people, because the use of drum by the Mizo is not new for them. It played an important role from their ancestors in many occasions especially at the time of festivals.

Although, the missionary did not encourage the use of drum in the church, the revival of 1919 brings the drum in the church service. Therefore, in the words of Lalsangkima, "despite disapproving cautions of the missionaries such as Llyod's, the drum became one of the distinctive marks of the Mizo Christian identity."[41] Now the drum is used in every church service in Mizoram. Therefore, Lalsawma compares Mizo church worship service without drum with "a dish of food without salt in it."[42]

Songs

After the first revival in 1906, the Mizo society experienced the introduction of *Puma Zai* (Songs of Puma). According to Liangkhaia, *Puma Zai* was originated from Ratu village. In March 1908, Chief Lalzika of Zawngin village celebrated *Puma Zai* with a great public feasts and continued for many days with singing and dancing. Some other chiefs also prepared feasts to celebrated *Puma Zai* by killing animals. Here, in the introduction of *Puma Zai*, elements

> All the major characteristics of the revival dance we have noted the waving and clapping of hands, the swaying of bodies and the circular movement-have their counter parts in the popular *Tlanglam*. Secondly, it should be noted that hundreds of converts in the 1920s and 1930s belonged to the generation that had wholeheartedly participated in the *Tlanglam*.[68]

Another common feature of the revival was singing and dancing the whole night. The Christians did not introduce this practice. In the discussion on the celebration of *Chapchar Kut* in the previous chapter, we know that the *Chai* party should be singing and dancing the whole first night as a custom. Hence, we may say that Christians expressed their feeling of merriment in a way with which they were familiar when they sing and dance the whole night.[69]

Public Feasts

One of the characteristics of the traditional festivals was the public feasts, which is a combination of both social and religious practices. Likewise, the slaughter of domestic animals to glorify God and giving feast for the public was the adaptation of traditional Mizo practices of *Thangchhuah* feasts.[70] In the old days, the wealthy family gave public feasts; the Christians now gave it to glorify God in an expression of joy. Till the early sixties revival feasts were so much common that they may well be included as a feature of the revival. Although, it is now less popular because of social change, many villages still practice this system. Lorrain notes;

> In this district the Christians often kill a domestic animal "to the glory of God" and give a feast to their neighbours. Some may think that it would be better if they sold the animal and gave the money to the church funds, but they have not reached that stage of development out of love to the savior do tend to glorify God's name and extended His Kingdom.[71]

Lawm Vawk which means "a pig kill to glory God" would be killed according to the means of the person and the size of the crowd expected. This feast was extended to all who would like to come both from the locality and surrounding localities.

Introduction of Christian Festivals

With the introduction of western Christianity all the traditional feasts and festivals were turned into a dry experience for the Mizo. Instead the missionaries demanded regular church attendance on Sunday for the new converts. As we have mentioned in the previous chapter, when Christianity spread, with the conversion from animism to Christianity, the Mizo begun to observe number of Christian festivals like Christmas, New Year, and Good Friday festivals.

Christmas

Christmas is celebrated on December 25 every year. This is the major Christian festival celebrated by the Mizo. Some of the important elements of the Christmas festival are worship, singing and dancing, and feasts.

The date and place of the first celebration of Christmas by the Mizo is still debatable. According to Darkunga for the first time the students celebrated Christmas in its Christian fashion in 1899 at Aizawl.[72] Till 1912 the celebration was reserved to only school children. It seems the missionaries and early Christians celebrated Christmas with their relatives and friends. J. M. Lloyd writes, "The church statistics in 1903 show that there were 46 communicant members in North and South. Eleven of these were Khasis; the rest Mizos. Naturally, being so few, there was a strong bond between them. As far as possible they celebrated Christmas together as one family."[73] The first public celebration of Christmas took place in 1913.[74] However, the account of Lalnghinglova, a senior minister from Presbyterian Church is differing from Darkunga's account. According to Lalnghinglova, the first Christmas celebration was hosted at Aizawl in 1905 in the presence of Rev. D. E. Jones and Rev. and (Mrs.) Edwin Rolands. Challiana's account tells us the Christmas was celebrated first in Lunglei in 1901,[75] while Lalnghinglova believed that the first Christmas celebration at Lunglei, South Mizoram was in 1912, under the patronage of Dahrawk Suaka, Chief of Durtlang village.[76]

One of the Mizo profile writers C. Laitanga observes that the missionaries did not make Christmas too much religious. They celebrated with fun and games. He believes that the present celebration of Christmas is too much religious. So that, some people regarded killing of animals on Christmas day as taboo.[77] On the other hand, another Mizo writer, M. Lalmanzuala argued the above discussion by saying, "as Christmas was for the day of worship to God, we should not celebrate with merriment and feast on this day."[78] As there are different ideas on the celebration of the Christmas day, the Mizoram Presbyterian Church (biggest church in Mizoram) Synod meeting of 1993 regarded that it is necessary to have guideline for the celebration by the church. The Synod entrusted the Synod Executive Committee, which formulated the guidelines. The guidelines says, "Christmas should be observed as Sunday by having morning, afternoon and night worship service to God" and the guidelines also say, "those who want to prepare feast, it is better to prepare feast on another date than Christmas day."[79] Therefore, the Presbyterian Churches in Mizoram celebrate Christmas according to the guidelines framed by the Synod. As we have discussed earlier the traditional festivals faded out after Christianity arrived in Mizoram. As timing of *Pawl Kut* coincides with Christmas, then Christmas became the major festival in Mizoram.

New Year

New Year festival is another important Christian festival celebrated by the Mizo Christian. This festival lasted for one or two days celebration with the church services and feasts. It depends upon the local church leaders and the congregation. Church service is held on this day and the congregation offers the drop to the church in thanking to God who blessed them with a good harvest.

Churches observed this festival with community feast by killing domestic animals. Some churches collected rice-flour, boiled it and distributed to the congregation for the refreshment after the morning service. This was called "*Chhang Ruai*" which means "feast with flour-rice."

Good Friday

Good Friday is also another important festival observed by the church. Church services, Holy Communion, singing and dancing are the chief elements of this festival. Good Friday festival was not observed as the Christmas festivals' "because the pioneering missionaries and their followers did not regard them as important as they did Christmas."[80] A popular saying has evolved that 'seeds sown on Good Friday yields better fruits' (*Good Friday ni a thlai chi lin chu a tha duh bik*). At present, the day is observed like a Sunday. The church conducted worship services three times, in the morning, afternoon and evening. In the interval of the church service, they gather together for singing and dancing. The entire sermon preached by the local pastors and the church elders were based on the passion story, the death and resurrection of Jesus. The church observed Good Friday as the day for the remembrance of the passion and death of Jesus.

Concluding Remarks

As we have seen the Christian festivals replaced the Mizo traditional festivals. Nevertheless, the spirit of the traditional festivals could still be seen in the Christian festivals. As Christianity rooted in the life of the people, these Christian festivals also rooted in the church as well as in the government. Therefore, the government announces holiday for all offices, schools and colleges to celebrate these festivals.

End Notes

1 H. Richard Neihbur, *Christ and Culture* (New York: Harper & Brothers Publishers, 1956), 33.

2 Yeow Choo Lak is Dean of the South East Asia Graduate School of Theology and Executive Director of the Association for Theological Education in South East Asia.

3 Yeow Choo Lak, "Christ in a Multi-Cultural Context," in *The Asia Church in the New Millennium*, edited by Raul Fernandez-Calienes (Delhi: ISPCK, 2000), 166.

4 Asenla, et al., "Gospel and Tribal Culture: Naga Perspective," in *Good News For North East India A Theological Reader*, edited by Renthy Keitzar (Guwahati: The Christian Literature Centre, 1995), 160.
5 Lalsangkima Pachuau, "Kristianna leh Mizo Culture," *Kum Sangbi Thara Mizo Kristianna Bihchianna* (Aizawl: Mizo Theological Association, 2003), 22.
6 N. E. Parry, *The Lakhers*, reprint (Calcutta: Firma KLM Private Ltd, 1976), 22.
7 Lalsawma, "Kristianna leh Hnam Culture," *Thu leh Hla* 20/3 (March, 1994): 2.
8 Lalrimawia, *Mizoram History and Cultural Identity* (Guwahati: Spectrum Publications, 1995), 125, 126.
9 McCall, *Lushai Chrysalis*, 207.
10 Hrangkhuma, "Mizoram Transforming Change," 210.
11 Chapman and Clark, *Mizo Miracle*, 120.
12 Lalrinawmi Ralte, *Upa Chalhnuna: Mizo Nun leh Kohhran* (Aizawl: Shalom Publications, 2009), 171.
13 Lalnghinglova, *Zoram Nghahchhan* (*Kristian Puipate leh an Thukhawchang*) (Aizawl: Saikungi, 1993), 7. Hereafter cited as Lalnghinglova, *Zoram Nghahchhan.*
14 Animish Ray, *Mizoram Dynamic of Change* (Calcutta: Pearl Publishers, 1982), 63.
15 Kipgen, *Christianity and Mizo Culture*, 315.
16 McCall, *Lushai Chrysalis*, 208.
17 Varghese and Thanzawna, *A History of the Mizos*, 327.
18 Hminga, *The Life and Witness of the Churches in Mizoram*, 295.
19 Mizo Presbytery 1910, Resolution No. 1.
20 Laldinliani Hrahsel, "A Study of the Educational Activities of Various Christian Denominations in Mizoram and their Impact on the Mizo Society" (Ph.D Dissertation, Mizoram University, 2000).
21 Zairema, *God's Miracle in Mizoram (A Glimpse of Christian Work among Head-Hunters)* (Aizawl: Synod Press & Book Room, 1978), 10. Hereafter cited as Zairema, *God's Miracle in Mizoram.*
22 Zaithanga, "A Study of Social and Cultural Changes Among the People of Mizo through the Impact of the Gospel" (BD Thesis, Senate of Serampore College University, 1964), 34.
23 Varghese and Thanzawna, *A History of the Mizos*, 322.
24 Zairema, *God's Miracle in Mizoram*, 11.
25 K. Lalrinmawia, "The Discourse on Zu (Alcoholic Beverages) in Mizo Christianity from 1894-1997)" (M. Th. Thesis, Senate of Serampore College University, 2002).
26 Lalnghakthuami, "Selected Mizo Festivals," 132.
27 Hminga, *The Life and Witness of the Churches in Mizoram*, 35.
28 Hluna, "Education in Mizoram…", 221, 222.

29 McCall, *Lushai Chrysalis*, 209.
30 Quoted in John Vanlalhluna, *Church and Political Upheaval in Mizoram* (Aizawl: Mizo History Association, 1985), 144.
31 Lalsangkima, *Ethnic Identity and Christianity*, 136.
32 Liangkhaia, *Mizo Chanchin*, 203.
33 Saiaithanga, *Mizo Kohhran*, 60.
34 Hminga, *The Life and Witness of the Churches in Mizoram*, 117.
35 Siama, *Mizo History*, 15.
36 Lalsawma, *Revivals-the Mizo Way*, 77.
37 Z. T. Sangkhuma, *Missionary-te Hnuhma* (Aizawl: M. C. Lalrinthanga, 1995), 163.
38 Lalrinawmi Ralte, "Dance Theology," *God's Image* 19/4 (December, 2000): 36.
39 Lalsangkima, *Ethnic Identity and Christianity*, 138.
40 Llyod, *History of the Church in Mizoram*, 192.
41 Lalsangkima, *Ethnic Identity and Christianity*, 139.
42 Lalsawma, *Revivals-the Mizo Way*, 79.
43 Saiaithanga, *Mizo Kohhran*, 29.
44 Lalsawma, *Revivals-the Mizo Way*, 48.
45 Hminga, *The Life and Witness of the Churches in Mizoram*, 74.
46 Zairema, *God's Miracle in Mizoram*, 18.
47 J. Meirion Llyod, *On Every High Hill* (Liverpool: Foreign Mission Office, n.d), 55. Hereafter cited as Lloyd, *On Every High Hill.*
48 Llyod, *History of the Church in Mizoram*, 108.
49 Saiaithanga, *Mizo Kohhran*, 28.
50 Liangkhaia, *Mizo Chanchin*, 196.
51 Cited in Lalsangkima, *Ethnic Identity and Christianity*, 119.
52 H. Remthanga, comp., *Synod Thurel Lak Khawm*, vol. I (1910-1950) (Aizawl: Synod Literature and Publication Board, 1996), 203.
53 Lloyd, *On Every High Hill*, 55.
54 Lalsangkima, *Ethnic Identity and Christianity*, 119.
55 Lalsangkima, *Ethnic Identity and Christianity*, 119.
56 B. Lalthangliana, *Mizo Literature* (Aizawl: M. C. Lalrinthanga, 1993), 132.
57 Kipgen, *Christianity and Mizo Culture*, 226.
58 Zawla, *Mizo Pi Pute leh An Thlahte Chanchin*, 403.
59 Hrangthiauva & Lalchungnunga, *Mizo Chanchin (History and Culture of the Mizos)* (Aizawl: Lalrinliana and Sons, 1978), 344. Hereafter cited as Hrangthiauva and Lalchungnunga, *Mizo Chanchin.*
60 Lalsangkima, *Ethnic Identity and Christianity*, 121.
61 Kipgen, *Christianity and Mizo Culture*, 232.
62 Kipgen, *Christianity and Mizo Culture*, 155.
63 Lalsangkima, *Ethnic Identity and Christianity*, 139.
64 Zairema, *God's Miracle in Mizoram*, 16.
65 Lalsangkima, *Ethnic Identity and Christianity*, 140.

66 Hminga, *The Life and Witness of the Churches in Mizoram*, 74.
67 Lalsangkima, *Ethnic Identity and Christianity*, 140.
68 Lalsangkima, *Ethnic Identity and Christianity*, 141.
69 Kipgen, *Christianity and Mizo Culture*, 275.
70 Kipgen, *Christianity and Mizo Culture*, 281.
71 Quoted by Kipgen, *Christianity and Mizo Culture*, 282.
72 Darkunga, "Krismas Hmasa Ber-Mizoramah," *Kristian Tlangau* xliv/519 (December, 1954): 278. Cited by Sangkima, *Mizos: Society and Social Change 1890-1947*, 144.
73 Llyod, *History of the Church in Mizoram*, 56, 57.
74 Sangkima, *Mizos: Society and Social Change 1890-1947*, 144.
75 Darchhawna, "Mizo Kutte leh Krismas (Pi Pute Hunpui (Kut) leh Krismas,)" *Kohhran Beng* 58/12 (December, 2003): 8.
76 Lalnghinglova, *Zoram Nghahchhan*, 117, 118.
77 C. Laitanga, "Mizo Society leh Social Customs and Practices," *Mizo Hnam Zia leh Khawtlang Nun Siam Thatna* (Aizawl: Synod Publication Board, 1988), 44.
78 Lalmanzuala, *Zoram Kalsiam-2* (Aizawl, Sapthlengliani, 1999), 75, 76.
79 *Presbyterian Handbook*, revised & enlarged (Aizawl: The Synod Publication Board, 1994), 59.
80 Sangkima, *Mizos: Society and Social Change 1890-1947*, 144

Chapter 5

Encounter Between Church and Culture Resurgence

This chapter deals with the encounter between the church and Mizo culture with the resurgence of *Chapchar Kut* in the middle of the twentieth century. It is an attempt to find why and how an attempt was made for the re-introduction of *Chapchar Kut* festival. The main focus will be the Mizoram Presbyterian church's response to the resurgence of the *Chapchar Kut* festival.

Attempt to Re-introduction of Traditional Culture

As we discussed in the previous chapter, it is very clear that the teaching of the missionaries took a deep root in the minds of the early Mizo Christians, and the influence is still among many of the church leaders in Mizoram particularly in the Mizoram Presbyterian Church. In the middle of the twentieth century, the church's attitude towards culture does not different from the early Christian leaders. On the other hand, with the introduction of education many educated Mizo came forward with the opinion that our cultural heritage should be re-introduced. The educated Mizo were determined to re-introduce the old traditional practices, which had been abandoned by the missionaries and the early Mizo Christians.

Talom Rukbo was one of the important leaders who wanted to preserve culture among the people of Arunachal Pradesh in North East India. According to him, under the rapid changes the young generation had forgotten traditional music, songs and dances. They know only music, songs and dances of 'advanced' society and play alien musical instruments. They do not believed in old faith, and ashamed to participate in traditional practices.[1] This statement is also true in Mizoram as the western life styles, dresses, music, songs and dances influenced the younger generations. The Mizo traditional practices were wiped out from the Mizo life till the middle of the twentieth century. After India's independence, with gradual development of the Mizo world view, there was a tendency to revive Mizo traditional festivals, folk songs and dances. Amit Kr. Nag, a Journalist, who had close contact with the Mizo, observes,

> The younger generation has been increasingly giving proofs of its desire for a cultural revival. Folk dances and music are in their initial stages of resurgence. The psychological complex which loomed largely mainly among the first generation of educated Mizos is becoming a thing of the past. Younger generations are learning to value and love their pre-literate culture, traditions and customs.[2]

Re-introduction of Chapchar Kut

After Indian independence, the administration of the Government was handed over to the native Mizo leaders in 1952, when the Mizo Hills was re-named as Mizo District. With the coming of the Mizo District Council, many of the fine aspects of the forgotten Mizo traditional cultures were re-introduced.

Around 1930, some Mizo staff in the office of the Superintendent applied for the celebration of *Chapchar Kut*. They celebrated *Chapchar Kut* at Thakthing Veng and Chaltlang.[3] In 1950 all the villages of Mizoram did not celebrate the *Chapchar Kut* festival. According to Khawvelthanga, a few Mizo who were longing for the old life celebrated the festival.[4] When the Mizo District Council was formed in 1952, steps were taken to revive the major traditional festivals. The Council had declared Government holidays for the celebration of Mizo traditional festivals *Chapchar Kut* (for 3 days), *Pawl Kut* (for 2 days) and *Mim Kut* (for 1 day).[5] Although, the Government declared the official holidays, public celebration of the festivals was started only from March 9, 1960 in an organized manner.[6] An Organizing Committee consisting of nine members was formed and Hrangaia, a member of the District Council was its convener. Other members were B. Poonte (Development Officer), Sangliana (Headmaster), Sainghinga (Chairman District Council Court), R. Buchhawna, R. Zuala, Tawnluia, Meli and Hmingliani. Therefore, under their leadership the annual celebration of *Chapchar Kut* was started at Aizawl, the capital. According to Lalsangkima Pachuau, "the attempt was not to revive the old festivals per se, but to commemorate them by symbolically exhibiting how the festival was celebrated in the past."[7]

On March 14, 1961 *Chapchar Kut* was celebrated in an organized manner and on a mass scale at the Assam Rifles parade ground in Aizawl. There were *Khuallam*, *Cheraw*, Hockey, *Inkawibah*, Cycle Races and Custom Parade to entertain the public. One journalist observes that the celebration of this year was 'the biggest gathering at Aizawl.'[8]

In 1962 and 1963, the *Chapchar Kut* celebration was held without any opposition from the Church. Instead, since, 1962 the celebration was "Symbolically Christianized by commencing each celebration with a ceremonial Christian prayer."[9] In March 1962 *Chapchar Kut* celebration, Christian Hymn "*Kan Pathian Kan Puipa Pangngai*" (O God, Our Help in Ages Past) was sung and Upa Vanchhunga offered a word of prayer. Different localities showed the Mizo cultural items like *Tlanglam*, *Chhawnghnawh*, *Chai*, *Cheraw*, *Khuallam*, *Khuangchawi* and Custom Parade. The celebration of the festivals went off very well until 1964 *Chapchar Kut* celebration.

In the 1964 *Chapchar Kut* celebration, without the knowledge of the organizers, some participants used bottles of rice-beer to ply the dancers. This became a hindrance for the future celebration of the festivals. Ch. Saprawnga, the then Council Executive Chief invited the church leaders and missionaries to discuss the matters. According to Hrangaia, although the missionaries and most of the leaders appeared to have understood the government's intent in celebrating the old festival, one of the most prominent Presbyterian leaders of the time Liangkhaia, resolutely objected and declared his dislikes to celebrate any occasion under the name of *Kut*. He, therefore, pleaded with the District Council never to do anything again under the name of *Kut* during his lifetime.[10] On the plea of Liangkhaia the Government stopped the celebration of *Chapchar Kut* in 1965. Thus, from 1965, the *Kut* celebrations were terminated, although a similar celebration was held on February 25, 1966 under the name *Zoram Ni* (Mizo day) instead of *Chapchar Kut*.[11] Lalsangkima Pachuau believed that Liangkhaia was the most influencial person at that time. He writes,

> He was such an influence to the Presbyterian Church that what he said and taught may almost be identified with the words and teachings of the Church. As stated above, when he asked the government not to do anything in the name of Mizo traditional *kut*, the District Government complied. His appeal indicates that he perceived traditional festivals as profane and that he held a negative attitude towards traditional culture and customary practices.[12]

During 1967-1971 there was no proper celebration of *Chapchar Kut* or *Zoram Ni* due to political disturbance in Mizoram. In 1972, the Mizo Student Association (Mizo Zirlai Pawl) General Assembly passed a resolution to renew commemorative celebration of the *Chapchar Kut*. At the same time, All Mizo Students Federation also passed the same resolution. The main key figure was Chuauthuama, the then General Secretary of the Mizo Student Association and the President of the All Mizo Students Federation. Leaders of the students discussed with Hrangaia and invited him to be the Chairman of the Organizing Committee. The Organizing Committee fixed the date for the celebration on March 7, 1973. The Information Department of the Government of Mizoram bared the expenses. The main question faced by the Organizing Committee were, "How shall we arrange the celebration in a way favourable to the Presbyterian Church Synod?" and "how shall we attract the public?"[13]

When the student leaders approached the Synod leaders, both the Synod Moderator and the Synod Secretary refused the Organizing Committee's invitation to solemnize the function. They also approached Lalsawma, the then Principal of the Aizawl Theological College, he also declined the invitation as both the Moderator and the Secretary had declined. When they approached the Chief Minister Ch. Chhunga, to preside over the opening ceremony, he bluntly replied "I could not accept the invitation unless the Presbyterian Church representatives promised to make their presence in the function."[14]

Till the morning of March 7, 1973, the Organizing Committee could not find a church leader to offer an opening prayer for the function. Around 9:00 o'clock in the morning, Lalsawma called back and reported that he was ready to offer an opening prayer for the function. "The student's invitation, he said, troubled him the whole night and felt he should not let them down."[15] Imagine their happiness, while they learnt this readiness of Lalsawma to offer a word of prayer at the function, while they had not found any other church leader. They informed the Chief Minister, Ch. Chhunga and accepted the invitation at once to officiate the opening ceremony of the *Chapchar Kut* celebration. Hence, with the present of Lalsawma, and then the Chief Minister Ch. Chhunga, *Chapchar Kut* was celebrated at A. R. Ground on a mass scale. Since that time, under the initiative of the Mizoram Government, the public celebration of the *Chapchar Kut* has been continued even today. "Even at this stage, the Church leaders were still not yet fully convinced but no opposition was voiced by them."[16]

There were the reasons for the successful celebration of the *Chapchar Kut* festival, in 1972, Mizoram was raised up to the status of a Union Territory. There were a popular rejoicing at the new political status and the formation of new government in Mizoram. On the other hand, the public was fed-up with the tense atmosphere of the independence movement declared by the Mizo National Front and they were yearning to relive their mental constriction through songs, dances and other worthwhile entertainment. In the words of Thanzawna,

> Under such condition, the Government of Mizoram was wise enough to find out ways and means of organizing such public entertainments and diversions. *Chapchar Kut* comes only once a year, what more can we do to create wholesome and peaceful atmosphere? Such entertainments will also go along way in bringing an end to the lingering insurgency and also bring about the spirit of cooperation and fraternity between the people-army, civil and Government servants, and perhaps wean back the insurgency too. With such ideas in mind, the Information and Public Relations Department under the leadership of the Chief Secretary organized Beat Contest, Recitation Competition, On-the-spot Painting Competitions and Winter Festivals on a grand scale. The results were amazing; the response from the public was simply great. Added to this, *Chapchar Kut* was organized on a grand scale, and at this stage the opposition from the church was not more than a caution.[17]

Before the state level Committee for *Chapchar Kut* celebration was formed with one senior officer of the Government as its Chairman. Since 1984 a permanent committee on *Chapchar Kut* Standing Committee was formed. The first Secretary of the Standing Committee was C. Laitanga. Under his leadership the celebration of the festival saw a lot of improvements. In this year the *Chapchar Kut* was celebrated not only in the state capital but also in many other villages. Hence, it may be called "Mizo Community festival." This shows that the *Chapchar Kut* celebration saw more improvement year by year.[18]

One of the important developments for the revival of cultural festivals was the creation of the Tribal Research Institute, which became the most important agent for the celebration of *Chapchar Kut*. Another important development was the existence of a separate Department of Art and Culture in Mizoram Government in 1989 in response to the sentiments of the young generations. All the properties and responsibilities of the *Chapchar Kut* Standing Committee were handed over to this department. Under the initiative of Art and Culture Department, *Chapchar Kut* celebrations were held every year till 1996.

Again, in 1996, the organizational responsibility for the celebration of *Chapchar Kut* was handed over to the Central Young Mizo Association (CYMA). Under the leadership of the CYMA the celebration became more extended, and included even all the Mizo who lived in other neighbouring states like Manipur and Tripura. Hence, *Chapchar Kut* celebration became the most important event for the building up of the Mizo identity. The celebration has become the most colourful cultural festival of Mizoram. The day is declared as State holiday by the State Government.

Although, we term it the *Chapchar Kut* festival, in reality, the celebration appears only to be in an adopted form and as a show piece of cultural heritage. It is not celebrated the way *Chapchar Kut* was really celebrated in the former days. Thus, the present day celebration is not the revival of the festival, rather it is meant only to commemorate or to preserve the cultural heritage of the Mizo.

As we had discussed earlier, although the Mizo District council try to renew all the three festivals, only the *Chapchar Kut* was revived to keep the cultural heritage. It is difficult to give the reason why only *Chapchar Kut* was re-introduced. The important question arising is whether the two festivals were more connected to the traditional religious beliefs and therefore clashes with the Christian teaching. L. B. Thanga says, "One could perhaps say that the last two being almost exclusively for worship of the divine beings relating agriculture, any attempt to revive these two would amount to renewal of nature worship, and it would no longer fit into our present day Christian life."[19] As we discussed earlier, all the three festivals were important in the life of the people, we also should give equal importance to the two other festivals not only the *Chapchar Kut*.

Church's Response to the Re-introduction of Chapchar Kut

In the previous chapter, we have dealt with the church's attitude towards the traditional festivals and other cultural activities in the early period of Christianity in Mizoram. The two largest denominations in Mizoram, the Mizoram Presbyterian Church and the Baptist Church of Mizoram, had the same attitude towards cultural revival. Both the churches "strongly discouraged their members from taking part in any of the *Kut* and cultural activities as they thought such activities would hold them and pull them back to their old pagan ways."[20] In fact, the Baptist Church had passed a resolution, in its Assembly meeting in the thirties, saying, "there is no harm to cultural activities and performance if it was merely done with the spirit of demonstration and not actual indulgence or adherence to the old animism."[21]

As we have discussed, the Presbyterian Church strongly discouraged its members from taking part in the revival of the *Chapchar Kut* and other cultural activities as they thought such activities would hold them and pull them back to their old pagan ways. The revival of *Chapchar Kut* festival was discussed at the Presbyteries and Synod meetings of the Mizoram Presbyterian Church. In 1962, the West Presbytery meeting resolved that, "The Synod should forbid old practices like *Chapchar Kut*, *Sechhun*[22] and *Khuangchawi*[23] which are not supposed to be practiced by Christians."[24] The Synod meeting of the same year had discussed the matter and referred the same back to the Pastorates and asked the Presbyteries to take up the matter.[25]

In 1963, the annual meetings of four Presbyteries, namely Chhimchhak,[26] Tuichangral,[27] Khawchhak[28] and Khawthlang[29] discussed the issue. Most of the Presbyteries except Tuichangral Presbytery had positive attitude towards the celebration of *Chapchar Kut*. Meanwhile, the Presbyteries expressed their desire that the celebration should not revive the "old" life. Therefore, the resolution of all these meetings showed that the Church did not make any attempt to stop the *Chapchar Kut* celebration. In the annual Synod meeting in 1963, the Mizoram Presbyterian Church had issued a disapproval of the celebration. The resolution read, "Christians are not to involve reviving the old culture and life style which they have renounced."[30]

When in 1964 celebration some participants used bottles of *zu* to ply the dancers, the Mizoram Presbyterian Church severely criticized the *Chapchar Kut* celebration. The Mizoram Presbyterian Church statement further says that church members should not allow their sons and daughters to join the *Chapchar Kut* celebration next time.[31]

While the celebration of the *Chapchar Kut* was organized on a large scale every year since 1973, an agenda was put for a discussion in the meeting of the Presbyterian Church Synod in 1975. The Synod meeting of 1975, discussed the resolution passed by the Hmarphei Presbytery. The resolution says, "Let the Synod explain clearly the compatibility and incompatibility between Christian life and traditional Mizo culture."[32] After a long discussion, the Synod meeting asked the Synod Executive Committee to take up the matter.[33] This shows that "tension continued, and the situation called for a new definition of the church's position."[34]

The Synod Executive Committee (SEC) meeting on September 1, 1976, took up the matter and discussed the Sub-committee's report. After a long discussion, the SEC reiterated the existing stance by saying that it was unnecessary to make a new rule on the matter because it was under the jurisdiction of local churches. Therefore, the SEC entrusted the local churches to decide what they feel as good on their respective locality.[35]

As the Presbyterian Church did not formulate any clear-cut rule in connection with the celebration of the *Chapchar Kut* festival, the different Presbyteries raise the same question to the Synod meeting from time to time. The Hmarchhak Presbytery put forward an agenda by suggesting "to Celebrate *Chapchar Kut* in Christian ways."[36] Therefore, the 1978, Synod meeting decided that the "involvement in *Kut* is disapproved by the Church."[37]

In 1984, the Khawchhak Presbytery asked the Synod to make a strict rule against some of the Mizo practice which are incompatible with Christianity like-*Chheih lam*, *Chai*, *Salu lam*, *Mi lu lam*, *Hla do*, *Sar lam* and *Puma zai*.'[38] After a long discussion the annual Synod meeting of the same year declared that, "Culture is an important element of ethnic identity which at the same time may also contain elements intolerable to the Church; therefore, we need a well-defined guideline."[39] The Synod meeting asked the Synod Executive Committee to prepare a definition on that matter to serve as a guide line. Then, the SEC nominated two respected Presbyterian leaders, Lalsawma and Lalngurauva Ralte to draft the guideline.[40] The Synod Executive Committee approved the guideline and was published in the form of a Press Release as follows.

Press Release on Mizo Traditional Culture

The Presbyterian Church Synod had discussed many times on the issue of the revival of the Mizo traditional culture in its meeting. As the confusion continues among its members even today, the annual Synod meeting of 1984, passed a resolution to make a guideline on this matter. As entrusted by the Synod, the Synod Executive Committee prepared a press on the guideline on as follows:

1. "Culture" means the way of life of the society, mode of living of the people and its connotations. Culture includes religion, economic, settlement, social life, dress, public entertainment and many others. No one survive without culture. Culture can be different from time to time because of the development of the environment or imported from other cultures. Therefore, this leads to a compatibility and incompatibility between the old and the new generation. In Mizoram, with the development and the influenced of other cultures, there are interaction between traditional culture and modern culture. This is because of we mixed up with the old culture and Christian cultures.
2. The old culture, which was incompatible with Christianity, was some of the old religious practices, which included festivals, old songs and dancing, and drinking of rice-beer. All these were banned by the new religion. On the other hand, economic, new standard of life, dresses and development, which were not forbidden by the new religion, brought some changes. Since the last thirty years, there has been an attempt to revive the old cultural

practices among the younger generation, which disturb members of the Church. Therefore, the Synod meeting of 1963 resolution says, "Christians are not to involve in reviving the old culture and life style which they have renounced."

3. The desire to revive traditional culture grew stronger year by year among younger generations. There are two main incentives to the revival of the tradition. One of these is a crane for worldly pleasure. They wanted to revive the old way: festivals, dances, old songs, and drinking as practiced in the olden days. This is incompatible with Christianity. The other incentive is the desire to prevent traditional culture from dying out and cultural show for the commemoration.
4. In this matter, the position of the church is still the same; cultural practices were restricted since they were incompatibles with the gospel of Christ. Till today, the Church disapproved to celebrate the festival without being compatible with the Gospel (cf. Prov. 26:11). But, if the celebration is only the commemoration of the old life and not to misguide the people, then the Church would agree on it (Rom. 12:1, 2).[41]

The above document explains the meaning of the term "culture" and it reaffirmed the Church's position of 1963, but it goes a step further to accommodate the commemorative celebration of *Chapchar Kut*. The document also acknowledges the emergence of the desire to revive traditional culture among the younger generation. The document also describes that there were two incentives for the revival of the traditional festival. The document shows that the first incentive wanted to revive the old lifestyles, which indulge themselves. The Church cannot accept this incentive. The second incentive, which was more acceptable than the first one, was to desire to prevent the traditional culture from dying out and celebrate only as "commemoration." The document clearly states that the Church agrees and accepts that if the revival of the traditional festival is the "commemoration" of the cultural practices in the old time.

When the Synod released its attitude towards traditional culture, it was difficult for the local church member to understand it. Therefore, the Tuichangral Presbytery put up another agenda to the Synod. The resolution says, "Let the Synod revise and edify the guideline on the involvement of Christian in *Chapchar Kut* celebration and Mizo culture."[42] The Synod meeting of 1992, agreed to revise the documents and asked the Synod Executive Committee to revise and distribute the revision to local churches.[43]

The Synod Executive Committee asked two respected leaders H. Remthanga and C. Rosiama to look into the matter and prepare a draft.[44] The next Synod Executive Committee meeting approved the draft on June 9-11, 1993. The following are the guidelines approved by the synod Executive Committee, which was distributed to each congregation.

1. The old practices of the Mizo culture like-festival, feast, dancing, singing and drinking, which are to be revived for the enjoyment, practiced by the non-Christian are very wordly. The Christians have to avoid these practices.
2. If the revival of the traditional culture is for the preservation and the commemoration of the old life, which does not misguide the people, it does not harm the Church. But if it is for the enjoyment with drinking of rice-beer and eating of meat, the Church members are not supposed to be involved in it.
3. In revitalizing the cultural practices, it is difficult to make boundary in detail for the Church. The worldly life, anything outspokenly immodest, and to hurt the feeling of someone is not in accord with the gospel. Therefore, Christians should use God-given conscience in this matter.
4. Traditional songs like *Puma Zai*, *Tlanglam Zai* and composed song with old tune, which is opposed to the church, should not be supported by the members of the Church.
5. With regards to the revitalizing of the Mizo culture, the position of the Church may be differing from place to place and it is inevitable to put in the same line. Therefore, the

> churches are requested to study the above points carefully so that each local church may follow the right path.

The document clearly shows that the church does not opposed to re-introduction of the traditional culture were mentioned in the press release issued by the church in 1985. It says, "if it is the commemoration of the cultural elements and do not misguide the people, then the church would agree on it."[45] The Church's attitude is same in the pamphlet distributed to all the churches by the Synod in 1993, it reads, "if the revival of the traditional culture is for the preservation and the commemoration of the old life, which does not misguide the people, it does not harm the church."[46] It is very clear that the Church's attitude towards Mizo traditional festivals and other cultural activities are positive, if the re-introduction does not connect with the old ways of life. On the other hand, the Church strongly discouraged its members from taking part in any attempt to re-introduce *Chapchar Kut* in connected with the old religion and the drinking of rice-beer.

While the above document is officially the position of the Church, the opinions of the leaders of the Church also changing from time to time. As we had discussed, Liangkhaia strongly opposed for re-introduction of *Chapchar Kut* festival in the beginning. But, Liangkhaia shifted his position later, which he clearly stated in his article "*Hla Thu*" published in *Mizo Zirlai Pawl Chanchin Bu* in 1973. In his article he writes, "The Mizo Christian Hymns were composed and arranged by the missionaries without having knowledge of the Mizo poetical words. We the early Christians believed that the Christian hymns should be like this and believed that the Mizo poetical words were connected with paganism. We now admitted we are wrong."[47] He further says, "The use of drum and poetical expression should have been welcomed a long time ago."[48]

Recent Development on the Issue

Mizoram Presbyterian Church's Notification on Chapchar Kut and Other Made up Festivals, 2019.

(Ref. 2018 Synod Gen. 38: SEC 279:27 of 19-21.2.19; OM 5:34 of 2019; OM 7:4 of 2019).

Mizoram Presbyterian Church from its formative days had made formal guidelines for the members regarding Festivals and Ethnic Culture. In spite of the changing times and contexts, although there are additions and modifications, the church remains firm in its stance. Since the Mizo were used to heavy drinking bouts during festivals and feasts which were connected with the old beliefs of the ancestors, the Zosaps (British missionaries) and earliest believers knew that they had no part to play in these festivities. However, around 1930, the non-Christian population had seek permission from the District Collector to celebrate these Mizo festivals. In 1952, the leaders of the Mizo District Council announced holidays on the occasions of *Mim Kut, Chapchar Kut* and *Pawl Kut* (the autumn, spring and harvest festivals).

In 1960, the governing District Council organized Chapchar Kut with prayer and leading role played by the Church under a smooth environment. In 1963, after taking opinions regarding *Chapchar Kut* and the old/traditional Mizo culturefrom the Presbyteries, it was resolved that "It is not the duty of Christians to revive the traditions of the ancestors which were already rejected." In 1978, with regard to *Chapchar Kut*, it was again resolved that "It is not good for the Church to take an active role." In 1984, in accordance with the Synod's resolution, the Synod Executive Committee (SEC) 97:10 stated that "...celebrating festivals with drinking revelry...is prohibited, whatever is not in accordance with the Gospel of Christ is not allowed even today (Prov. 26:11). However, it is not a concern for the church if it is simply an exhibition of the old culture and doesn't led the participantsa miss (Rom 12:1, 2)." In the Synod of 1992, guidelines for church members with regard to participation in *Chapchar Kut* and other Mizo festivals was reviewed and revised. Following this up, the SEC 135:14 made a Notification which said, "To revive *Kut* (festivals), *Chawngchen* (feast given by single individual/family), *Chai* (a Mizo merry dance), Singing, dancing and drinking bout just for the craving of the old ways and mere enjoyments are desires of the godless worldly persons. The faithful must abstain from these."

If these festivals etc. are organised because of "the craving of the old ways and mere enjoyments" the faithful are advised not to participate. With regard to *Kut*, depending on the manners of celebrations, the Church is becoming more open. Although, the church doesn't openly encourage it, if it is simply an exhibition of the old culture and doesn't lead the participants amiss, it also do not resent it.

As this is still the position of the church, in the last few years, many new frontiers in the livelihood of the people is opening up and floral business (especially in anthurium) has become the source of living for some people. And the state government in the meantime has made up more festivals to attract tourists in order to boost the economy.

There are three major categories of *Kut* (festivals) which are celebrated these days:

1. **Chapchar Kut**: This is organized by the State government annually.
2. **Mizo/Zofate Kut in the metropolitans of India**: *Thal Favang Kut* in Shillong, *Vangpui Kut* in Bengaluru, *Sikpui Kut* among the Hmar community, Zofest organized by the MZP (Mizo Zirlai Pawl/Mizo Student Association), and other festivals organized by the Mizo community in different cities across India for fostering unity and cooperation through games and sports.
3. **Other Made-up Festivals**: Anthurium Festival, *Kurtai* (a Mizo Jaggery). Festival, Grape Wine Festival, *Khawchhuak* Festival a festival in which immigrants and their descendants return to their native places.

In the 2018 Synod, the Aizawl East Presbytery put forward an agenda to "Let the Synod make notification again regarding *Chapchar Kut* and other Made-up *Kut*/festivals" and the Tuivai Presbytery also proposed that the "Synod should make clarification for the Mizos with regard to participations in made-up *kut* (festivals)." These two agendas were discussed together at the Synod and the Synod resolved that "the proposal is good and the SEC should further take up the matter."

The SEC 297:27 (19-21 February 2019) handover the matter to the Synod Officers' Meeting (OM) giving them the task to prepare the notification for public distribution. After a careful consideration, the OM 5/2019:34 made the following points for our members in regard to their participation in *Chapchar Kut* and other made-up festivals:

1. *Chapchar Kut*

Chapchar Kut is celebarted every year officially by the Government. The manners of celebrations during the formative years of the church in Mizoram and today now differs widely. Therefore, unlike the early days, the church doesn't opposed it fervently now. However, there are still areas of concern for the church members. We must remember the following points while celebrating *Chapchar Kut*:

(1) *Kut* (festivals) and drinking revelries because of the craving of the old ways and mere enjoyments are the desires of the godless worldly persons. The faithful must abstain from these (ref. *Synod Thurel Lak Khawm*/Collections of Synod Resolutions, Vol. IV P. 609, no 1, slightly modified).

(2) It is not a concern for the church if it is used for the preservation of the Mizo culture and doesn't lead the participants amiss. However if it is associated with drinking revelries, the church members should never take part in it (ref. ibid., no. 2).

(3) The church members should refrain from some recent indecencies during *Chapchar Kut* like drinking and taking other forms of intoxication, sex outside marriage and anything that can drift us away from God. In such a situation, the member must rather choose not to participate.

2. Mizo Festivals outside Mizoram

Outside of Mizoram, if the Mizo migrant workers and students celebrate their festivals without losing their Christian principles, refraining from intoxicants and immoral acts and not drifting away from God, such festivals need not be considered as a serious matter.

3. Other Made-up Festivals

The other made-up festivals mentioned above which are organized by the State government to attract tourists may be for the sake of development but it is better not to encourage them. These festivals have many adverse effects on individuals and families and instead of nurturing the souls, they are becoming more of an obstacle. If these occasions clashes with the important dates and services of the Church, the Church members must give more importance to the Church programmes.

The *Khawchhuak* (Home-based/village of origin) Welfares are good for cooperation during good times and bad times. Some welfare organizes "*Haw Runpui*" (An occasion of organized return to one's hometown) and "(A particular Village/Town) Festival." This kind of festivals based on a particular village/town have their own pros and cons. But, they should not clash their dates with church programmes. These kinds of festivals should be organized and guided with the Christian principles.

These different made-up festivals should not be used as opportunity for indulging with intoxicants, sex outside of marriage and worldly pleasure. If they are drifting us away from God, the faithful must not take part in them. We do not strictly opposed our members to take part in these made-up festivals but we encourage them not to popularize these festivals for it will be muchbetter for our spirituality.

The younger generation do not satisfied with the re-introduction of *Chupkar Kut*, different kinds of Kut are introducing like *Thalfavang Kut*, Anthurium *Kut*, *Sawhthing Kut*, and so on. Therefore, the Aizawl East Presbytery put up another agenda to the Synod. The resolution says, "Let the Synod revise and edify the guideline on the involvement of Christian in *Chapchar Kut* and other indigenous *kut* celebration."[49] And the Hmarchhak Presbytery put forward an agenda by suggesting "Let the Synod edify how far the Church members will involve in celebrating the indigenous *kut*."[50] The Synod meeting accepted the agendas and entrusted the Synod Executive Committee to do the needful.[51] Then, the SEC nominated two respected Presbyterian leaders, Lalsawma and Lalngurauva Ralte to draft the guideline.[52] The Synod Executive Committee approved the guideline and was published in the form of a Press Release as follows.

Even today, the re-introduction of *Chapchar Kut* festival is still debated among the people and the leaders of the church. While the old generations opposed the re-introduction of the festival, the young church leaders are more liberal yet ambivalent. These young church leaders saw no harm in singing the old songs, dancing the traditional cultural dances, if there were no drinking and pagan revelry and obeisance to anything connected to the old animism.

In the fast changing Mizo society, attitudes and values change as rapidly as does our environment. The enlightened Mizo society does not longer askance at our cultural heritage as detrimental to the integrity of our faith rather as an entertainment of Christian brotherhood worldwide. Hence, when the church choir performed within and abroad, they used to show cultural dances and sung the old traditional tune.

Concluding Remarks

We have seen how *Chapchar Kut* has been kept alive for the preservation of cultural heritage. Although, the Mizo celebrated the *Chapchar Kut* festival every year, the celebration was only for commemoration of the cultural heritage without having connection with the paganism. Therefore, the Church has agreed to celebrate the festival as it is a mere commemoration and does not harm to the church. We may say that there is no reason to hesitate to participate in the celebration of *Chapchar Kut* festival as we do today.

Chapchar Kut is still observed as the festival of gaiety and merriment and mass singing and dancing. Drinking of *zu* on festive occasions as was practiced in the early period was not entertained as Christian prohibited drinking of it. *Chapchar Kut,* however, is not observed in the village as it used to be earlier, but in the State and District headquarters under the initiatives of the Government it is observed as a Mizo national festival with the objective of preserving the old culture.

End Notes

1 Cited in Atul Chandra Talukdar, "Tribal Cultural Revival in Arunachal Pradesh," in *Impact of Christianity on North East India*, edited by J. Puthenpurakal (Shillong: Vendreme Institute Publications, 1996), 486.

2 Amit Kr. Nag, *Tribal Mirror, Vol. II* (Silchar: Tribal Mirror Publication, 1966), 85-86.

3 R. L. Thanzawna, "The Origin of *Chapchar Kut*," *Chapchar Kut Souvenir* (Aizawl: Chapchar Kut Organizing Committee, 2003), 43. Hereafter cited as Thanzawna, "Chapchar Kut".

4 Khawvelthanga, "Lung Hlui a Leng Mange," *Chapchar Kut Souvenir* (Aizawl: Chairman, Publicity & Literature Committee, Chapchar Kut, 1995), 42.

5 Mizoram District Council Rorel Inkhawm, October 1953, Resolution No. 4. *Zoram Hriattirna* (Zoram Herald) (December, 1952), 11.

6 Hrangaia, "Chapchar Kut Lammuala Mipuite Hman Tan Dan," *Chapchar Kut* (Aizawl: Chapchar Kut Committee, 1985), 6. Hereafter cited as Hrangaia, "Chapchar Kut".

7 Pachuau, *Ethnic Identity*, 103.

8 *Mizo Arsi, Daily News Paper*, March 16, 1961. See B. Lalthangliana, "Chapchar Kut Uar Thar leh Dan," *Chapchar Kut Souvenir* (Aizawl: Chapchar Kut Organizing Committee, 2003), 9.

9 Pachuau, *Ethnic Identity*, 103.

10 R. Vanlawma, "Chapchar Kut" *Chapchar Kut Souvenir* (Aizawl: Chapchar Kut Committee, 1978), 26.

11 Hrangaia, "Chapchar Kut," 8.

12 Lalsangkima, *Ethnic Identity and Christianity*, 104.

13 Lalsangkima, *Ethnic Identity and Christianity*, 105.

14 Cited in Lalthangliana, "Chapchar Kut," 10.

15 Lalsangkima, *Ethnic Identity and Christianity*, 105.

16 Thanzawna, "Chapchar Kut," 47.

17 Thanzawna, "Chapchar Kut," 47, 48.

18 Lalthangliana, "Chapchar Kut," 11.

19 L. B. Thanga, "Culture and Its Heritage," *Chapchar Kut Souvenir* (Aizawl: Chairman, Publicity & Literature Sub-Committee, Chapchar Kut, 1995), 53.

20 Thanzawna, "Chapchar Kut," 46.

21 Quoted by Thanzawna, "Chapchar Kut," 46.

22 Sechhun/Sechhaih: The sport of chasing a gayal from place to place before it is sacrificed. Generally this is accompanied by great cruelty. The victim being a domesticated animal and often very docile it may need much beating and other mal-treatment to make it run fast enough to please its shouting tormentors, who hang on to its tether hounding it from place to place for hours, and sometimes for days. Occasionally the poor animal is subjected to such terrible cruelty that it dies before it can be sacrificed. Lorrain, *Dictionary of the Lushai Language*, 412.

23 Khuangchawi: Khuangchawi is the name of public feast given by Chiefs and other well-to-do Lushais.
24 West Presbytery Resolution No. 7 of 1962.
25 Synod Resolution No. 7 of 1962.
26 Chhiamchhak Presbytery Resolution No. 8 of 1963.
27 Tuichangral Presbytery Resolution No. 5 of 1963.
28 Khawchhak Presbytery Resolution No. 10 of 1963.
29 Khawthlang Presbytery Resolution No. 5:10 of 1963.
30 Synod Resolution Gen. 1 of 1963.
31 B. Lalthangliana, "Chapchar Kut," 9.
32 Hmarphei Presbytery Meeting Minute, 1975.
33 Synod meeting Minute, 1975:V:40.
34 Lalsangkima, *Ethnic Identity and Christianity*, 106.
35 Synod Executive Committee Meeting Minute, 41:5 (a) of September 1, 1976.
36 Hmarchhak Presbytery Meeting Minute, 1978.
37 Synod Meeting Minute, 1978:V:32.
38 Khawchhak Presbytery meeting Minute, 1984.
39 Synod Meeting Minute, IV: Gen. 18 of 1984.
40 Synod Executive Committee Minute, 93:8 of 10. 12. 1984.
41 Synod Executive Committee Minute, 97:10 of 6.11.1985.
42 Tuichangral Presbytery Minute, 1992.
43 Synod Meeting Minute, IV:52 of 1992.
44 Synod Executive Committee Minute, 134:13 of 17-20. 2. 1993.
45 Synod Executive Committee Minute, 97:10 of 6.11.1985.
46 Synod Executive Committee Minute, 135:14 of June 9-11, 1993.
47 Quoted by Z. T. Sangkhuma, *Missionary–te Hnuhma* (Aizawl: M. C. Lalrinthanga, 1995), 206.
48 Cited in Lalsangkima, *Ethnic Identity and Christian.*
49 Aizawl East Presbytery Meeting Resolution No. Gen 3.
50 Hmarchhak Presbytery Meeting Minute No.
51 Synod 2018 Resolution Gen No. 38.
52 Synod Executive Committee Resolution no. 279/27.

Conclusion

In the early period of Mizo history, festivals, rites and ceremonies were unpolutted by wetern influence and were deserving of promotion and protection. In the life of our forefathers, all the main principal of traditional festivals like *Chapchar Kut*, *Mim Kut* and *Pawl Kut* were important. These festivals were really connected with the socio, political, economic and religious life of the people.

With the annexation of the land by the British, Christianity followed the colonial flag in Mizoram as in the other land of the country. The Protestant Christian missionsries started coming to the land from the last decade of of the nineteenth century. With the sincere service they rendered, they won the heart of the Mizo to accept Christianity as their religion. Within a short period of time, most of the Mizo became Christians.

We know that the missionary goal, which is, retaining "all that is good in Mizo life while following on to what is better," was not really achieved. Most of the missionaries came without having knowledge of the indigenous elements. Their main aim was to preach the Gospel and to win over the native to Christianity. As there was no option for the early Mizo Christians, they adopted Christianity as their religion. With the influence of the Western culture, the early Mizo Christians discarded most of their indigenous cultural heritages like the traditional tunes for the songs and the use of drum. They, therefore, rejected anything, which was perceived to be associated with the old culture and the animism.

From our discussion we came to know that Christianity had brought a radical change in the socio-religious practices of the Mizo. Of these three festivals, *Chapchar Kut* is still observed as the festival of gaiety and merriment and mass singing and dancing, the two festivals, *Mim Kut* and *Pawl Kut*, are no longer observed. Drinking or rice-beer on festive occasions as was practiced before is no longer in vogue as Christianity prohibits. *Chapchar Kut*, however, is not observed in the village as used to be before, but in the state and District headquarters under the initiatives of the government as a Mizo national festival with the objective of preserving the old culture from dying.

We also came across that there are a number of other pre-christian cultural elements of the traditional festivals still surviving among the Mizo like singing and dancing the whole night, drum and community feasts were adopted in the celebration of the Christian festivals like Christmas, New Year and Good Friday. In other words, the traditional festivals were reintroduced in another form, which the Mizo Christians do not realize. Thus, one may find the similarity of the nature of festivals and the forms in which they had been shaped.

It is crystal clear that the Church attititude to the traditional festivals has changed from the old generation to the younger generation. The early Church felt that most of the cultural traditions of the heathens Mizo, including the obersvance of *Chapchar Kut* and other *kuts*, which were so profusely connected with animistic practices and drinking of rice-beer, were unbecoming of Christian living. Hence, the Church in its first meeting in 1910, forbade the new converts to participate and indulge in the festivals. As we live in the changing society, the attitude of the Church is also changing. In our study we know that, the Church attitude to the cultural elements, in particular the re-introduction of *Chapchar Kut* festival was also changing from meeting to its meeting. In the first decade of the twentieth century, the Church did not accept any celebration of festivals, which was connected with the old religious beliefs. But, in the last decade of the twentieth century, the Church accepted the re-intoduction of a festival if it was only for the commomeration and preservation of cultural heritage.

We may conclude that there was no harm in singing the old songs, dancing the traditional cultural dances, if there were no drinking of rice-beer and anything connected to the old animism.

With the passes of time, the younger generation tries to Christianize the celebration of the Mizo festivals. Here, I would like to propose or recommend for the celebration of *Chapchar Kut* and other *kuts*.

Decentralization of the Celebration of the *Chapchar Kut* Festival

We know that the Government of Mizoram centralizes the celebration of *Chapchar kut* in the state capital and district capitals. Hence, the festival could not become popular festival among the rural people because only the inhabitants of the state and district capital can celebrate the festival. Most of the villagers never participated in the celebration. Moreover, it seems in the present situation, should the Government fail to bear the expenses the celebration would not be possible.

If the celebration is decentralized and celebrated in every village under the initiatives of the Village Council or Young Mizo Association, the celebration may be more meaningful and the church's involvement also would be possible. In our present celebration, the church never involves herself in the committee. If the celebration is decentralized in the villages, the village leaders and the church leaders can discussed together the mode of celebrating the festival compatible with Christianity.

Integrating the Traditional Festivals with the Christian Celebration

The Mizo Christian community (ever hardly) never integrated their cultural heritage into their worship/religious rites or rituals or celebration. The cultural/traditional festivals were celebrated per se merely as commemoration of the cultural heritage. In the history of Judiasm, we learned that most of their important festivals were the

Presbytery Minutes

West Presbytery Meeting Minute No. 7 of 1962.

Chhiamchhak Presbytery Meeting Minute No. 8 of 1963.

Tuichangral Presbytery Meeting Minute No. 5 of 1963.

Khawchhak Presbytery Meeting Minute No. 10 of 1963.

Khawthlang Presbytery Meeting Minute No. 5:10 of 1963.

Hmarphei Presbytery Meeting Minute, 1975.

Hmarchhak Presbytery Meeting Minute, 1978.

Khawchhak Presbytery meeting Minute, 1984.

Tuichangral Presbytery Minute, 1992.

Aizawl East Presbytery Meeting Resolution No. 3 of 2018

Hmarchhak Presbytery Meeting Minute No. of 2018.

B. Government Documents

Resolution No. 4 in the Proceeding of the Hills Officers' Conference held at Shillong on July 21, 1937.

N. K. Rustomji, Adviser to the H. E. the Governor of Assam for Excluded Areas and States Letter D. O. No. 59/48/C-247-245, Shillong, the 17th February, 1949 to the Superintendent, Lushai Hills.

L. L. Peters, Superintendent, Lushai Hills Letter D. O. No. 15597/C, Aijal 23-2-1949 to N. K. Rustomji, Adviser to H. E. the Governor of Assam for Excluded Areas and States, Shillong.

Mizoram District Council Rorel Inkhawm, October 1953, Resolution No 4. *Zoram Hriattirna* (Zoram Herald) (December, 1952.

Census 2001, xxix.

C. Books

Bowser, M. Eleanor. *Light on the Lushai Hills: The Story of a Dream that Come True*. London: The Carey Press, n.d.

Carter, H. W. *Chhim Bial Kohhran Chanchin*. Serkawn: Rev. H. W. Carter, 1945.

Challiana. *Pi Pu Nun*. Aizawl: Lalrinliana & Sons, 1987.

Chapman, E. & M. Clark. *Mizo Miracle*. Edited by Marjorie Skyes. Madras: The Christian Literature Society, 1968.

Chatterjee, Suhas. *Mizoram under the British Rule*. New Delhi: Mittal Publication, 1985.

Downs, Frederick S. *Christianity in North East India*. Delhi: ISPCK, 1983.

Hminga, Chhangte Lal. *The Life and Witness of the Churches in Mizoram*. Serkawn: Literature Committee, Baptist Church of Mizoram, 1987.

Hrangthiauva & Lalchungnunga. *Mizo Chanchin (History and Culture of the Mizos)*. Aizawl: Lalrinliana and Sons, 1978.

Jeyakumar, D. Arthur. *Christians and the National Movement, The Memoranda of 1919 and the National Movement with Special reference to Protestant Christians in Tamil Nadu: 1919-1939.* Calcutta: Punthi Pustak, 1999.

Kipgen, Mangkhosat. *Christianity and Mizo Culture*. Aizawl: Mizo Theological Conference, 1997.

Lalkhawliana and C. Sangzuala, ed. *Mizoram Gospel Centennial Jubilee-1994*. Aizawl: The Gospel Centenary Sub-Committee on Souvenir for and on behalf of the Mizoram Presbyterian Church Synod, n.d.

Lalmanzuala. *Zoram Kalsiam- 2*. Aizawl, Sapthlengliani, 1999.

Lalnghinglova. *Zoram Nghahchhan* (*Kristian Puipate leh an Thukhawchang*). Aizawl: Saikungi, 1993.

Lalrimawia. *Mizoram History and Cultural Identity*. Gauhati: Spectrum Publications, 1995.

Lalrinthanga, H. *Church and State Relationship in the Mizo Socio-Political Life 1952-2006*. Delhi: ISPCK, 2013.

Lalsawma. *Revivals-the Mizo Way*. Aizawl: The Author, 1994.

Lalthangliana, B. *Mizo Literature*. Aizawl: M. C. Lalrinthanga, 1993.

Liangkhaia. *Mizo Chanchin*, 5th ed. Aizawl: L.T.L. Publication, 2002.

Lloyd, J. Meirion. *History of the Church in Mizoram, Harevest in the Hill*. Aizawl: Synod Publication Board, 1991.

Llyod, J. Meirion. *On Every High Hill.* Liverpool: Foreign Mission Office, n.d.

Lorrain, J. H. *Dictionary of the Lushai Language*, 4th reprint. Calcutta: The Asiatic Society, 1997.

Lorrain, Reginald A. *Five Years in unknown Jungles.* London: Lakher Pioneer Mission, 1912.

McCall, Anthony Gilchrist. *Lushai Chrysalis.* London: Lusac & Co., Limited, 1949.

Nag, Amit Kr. *Tribal Mirror, Vol. II.* Silchar: Tribal Mirror Publication, 1966.

Nag, Chitta Ranjan. *The Mizo Society in Transition.* New Delhi: Vikash Publishing House Pvt. Ltd., 1993.

Pachuau, Lalsangkima. *Robert Arthington-a leh a Ramthar Rawngbawlna Chanchin* (Robert Arthington and His Foreign Missions). Aizawl: Synod Publication Board, 1994.

Pachuau, Lalsangkima. *Ethnic Identity and Christianity.* Frankfrut: Peter Lang, 2002.

Parry, N. E. *The Lakhers.* Reprint. Calcutta: Firma KLM Private Ltd, 1976.

Parry, N. E. *A Monograph on Lushai Customs and Ceremonies.* Reprinted. Shillong: Ri Khasi Offset Printers, 1988.

Presbyterian Handbook. Revised & enlarged. Aizawl: The Synod Publication Board, 1994.

Ralte, Lalrinawmi. *Upa Chalhnuna: Mizo Nun leh Kohhran.* Aizawl: Shalom Publications, 2009.

Ray, A. C. *States of Our Union Mizoram.* Delhi: Publications Division, Ministry of Information and Broadcasting Government of India, 1972.

Ray, Animish. *Mizoram Dynamic of Change.* Calcutta: Pearl Publishers, 1982.

Remthanga, H., comp. *Synod Thurel Lak Khawm.* Vol. I (1910-1950). Aizawl: Synod Literature and Publication Board, 1996.

Saiaithanga. *Mizo Sakhua.* Aizawl: Maranatha Press, 1984.

Saiaithanga. *Mizo Kohhran Chanchin.* 3rd print. Aizawl: The Mizo Theological Literature Committee, 1993.

Sangkhuma, Z. T. *Missionary-te Hnuhma.* Aizawl: M. C. Lalrinthanga, 1995.

Sangkima. *Mizos: Society and Social Change 1890-1947.* Guwahati: Spectrum Publications, 1992.

Shakespear, J. *The Lusei Kuki Clan.* Part I. Aizawl: Tribal Research Institute, 1975.

Spencer, Anand. *Understanding Religion: Theories and Methodology.* Patiala: Vision and Venture, 1997.

Strom, Donna. *Wind through the Bamboo: The Story of Transformed Mizo.* Reprint. Madras: Evangelical Literature Service, 1991.

Thanga, Selet. *Pi Pu Lenlai,* 13th ed. Aizawl: Lianchhungi Book Store, 1990.

Thanzauva, K., comp. *Reports of the Foreign Mission of the Presbyterian Church of Wales on Mizoram 1894-1957.* Aizawl: The Synod Literature and Publication Boards, 1997.

Vanlalhluna, John. *Church and Political Upheaval in Mizoram.* Aizawl: Mizo History Association, 1985.

Vumson, *Zo History.* Aizawl: The Author, n.d.

Zairema. *God's Miracle in Mizoram (A Glimpse of Christian Work among Head-Hunters).* Aizawl: Synod Press & Book Room, 1978.

Zu in Mizo Society (*Past and Present*) Aizawl: Senior Research Officer, Tribal Research Institute, 1983.

D. Articles

Asenla, et al. "Gospel and Tribal Culture: Naga Perspective." In *Good News For North East India A Theological Reader.* Edited by Renthy Keitzar. Guwahati: The Christian Literature Centre, 1995.

Laitanga, C. "Mizo Society leh Social Customs and Practices." *Mizo Hnam Zia leh Khawtlang Nun Siam thatna.* Aizawl: Synod Publication Board, 1988.

Lak, Yeow Choo. "Christ in a Multi-Cultural Context." In *The Asia Church in the New Millennium*. Edited by Raul Fernandez-Calienes. Delhi: ISPCK, 2000.

Neihbur, H. Richard. *Christ and Culture*. New York: Harper & Brothers Publishers, 1956.

Pachuau, Lalsangkima. "Kristianna leh Mizo Culture." *Kum Sangbi Thara Mizo Kristianna Bihchianna*. Aizawl: Mizo Theological Association, 2003.

Talukdar, Atul Chandra. "Tribal Cultural Revival in Arunachal Pradesh." In *Impact of Christianity on North East India*. Edited by J. Puthenpurakal. Shillong: Vendreme Institute Publications, 1996.

Taylor, Edward B. "Animism." In *Reader in Comprehensive Religion An Anthropological Approach*. 3rd ed. Edited by William A. Lessa and Evon Z. Vogt. New York: Harper & Row Publishers, 1972.

Zairema. "The Mizos and their Religions." *Towards A Tribal Theology: the Mizo Perspective*. Edited by K. Thanzauva. Jorhat: Mizo Theological Conference, 1989.

E. Unpublished Thesis/Dissertation/Paper

Fanai, Hrangkhuma. "Mizoram Transformational Change: A Study of the Process and Nature of Mizo Cultural Change and Factors that Contributed to the Change." Ph.D Dissertation, Fuller Theological Seminary, 1989.

Hrahsel, Laldinliani. "A Study of the Educational Activities of Various Christian Denominations in Mizoram and their Impact on the Mizo society." Ph.D Dissertation, Mizoram University, 2000.

Lalrinmawia, K. "The Discourse on Zu (Alcoholic Beverages) in Mizo Christianity from 1894-1997)." M.Th. Thesis, Senate of Serampore College University, 2002.

Lalrinthanga, H. *Church and State Relationship in the Mizo Socio-Political Life 1952 to 2006*. Delhi: ISPCK, 2013.

Pachuau, Lalsangkima."Mizo Sakhua Then and Now: Change and Continuity between Mizo Primal Religion and Mizo Christianity." Faculty Research Seminar paper, UTC, November 12, 2003.

Zaithanga, V. L. "A Study of Social and Cultural Changes among the People of Mizo through the Impact of the Gospel." B. D. Thesis, Senate of Serampore College, 1964.

F. Souvenir

Hrangaia. "Chapchar Kut Lammuala Mipuite Hman Tan Dan." *Chapchar Kut Souvenir*. Aizawl: Chapchar Kut Committee, 1985.

Khawvelthanga. "Lung Hlui a Leng Mang e." *Chapchar Kut Souvenir*. Aizawl: Chairman, Publicity & Literature Committee, Chapchar Kut, 1995.

Lalthangliana, B. "Chapchar Kut Uar Thar leh Dan." *Chapchar Kut Souvenir*. Aizawl: Chapchar Kut Organizing Committee, 2003.

Thanga, L. B. "Culture and Its Heritage." *Chapchar Kut Souvenir*. Aizawl: Chairman, Publicity & Literature Sub-Committee, Chapchar Kut, 1995.

Thanzawna, R. L. "The Origin of Chapchar Kut." *Chapchar Kut Souvenir*. Aizawl: Chapchar Kut Organizing Committee, 2003.

Vanlawma, R. "Chapchar kut." *Chapchar Kut Souvenir*. Aizawl: Chapchar Kut Committee, 1978.

G. Journals

Darchhawna. "Mizo Kutte leh Krismas (Pi Pute Hunpui (Kut) leh Krismas)." *Kohhran Beng* 58/12 (December, 2003): 8.

Darkunga. "Krismas Hmasa Ber-Mizoramah." *Kristian Tlangau* xliv/519 (December, 1954): 278.

Lalsawma. "Kristianna leh Hnam Culture." *Thu leh Hla* 20/3 (March, 1994): 2.

Ralte, Lalrinawmi. "Dance Theology." In *God's Image* 19/4 (December, 2000): 36.